Contents

KV-639-122

We should like to express our grateful thanks to the following people:

Aylestone Science Club, for doing the experiments
Shula, for typing them
Abdul and Naren, for corrections
as well as
Sylvia, Max and Bruce Temple
Sandra Banfield
and Richard 'Greenfingers' Kew

P.T.
R.L.
April 1982

How to Make
SQUARE
EGGS

Paul Temple and Ralph Levinson

Illustrated by David Mostyn

Beaver Books

First published in 1982 by
The Hamlyn Publishing Group Limited
London · New York · Sydney · Toronto
Astronaut House, Feltham, Middlesex, England
Reprinted 1983

© Copyright Text Paul Temple
and Ralph Levinson 1982
© Copyright illustrations
The Hamlyn Publishing Group Limited 1982
ISBN 0 600 20456 1

Printed and bound in Great Britain by
Cox & Wyman Limited, Reading
Set in Bembo

Introduction

This is a book you won't believe. It's all about science and so there are plenty of experiments for you to do and think about. What's unusual is that each one is strange or ridiculous. Are there really square tomatoes? Of course there are. They fit nicely into square sandwiches. And wouldn't it be nice to have a bath without getting wet? Well, this book will show you square tomatoes, dry water and many other unbelievable things. The experiments are all safe for you to do. Most of them are easy to perform at home, but there are a few you will have to do at school. These start on page 91, and in addition to the star rating mentioned below, are indicated by an 'S'. Just ask your teachers if you can do them and you'll probably find they enjoy them as much as you.

Always remember that science is fun but you must be careful. Wash your hands after experiments which use chemicals. Never cut anything towards you and keep your clothes and hair out of the way, especially if you are near a flame. Follow our instructions carefully and read them right through before you start. Remember, it will make it easier if you have everything to hand before you begin. The glossary at the back of the book explains words you may not have come across before.

Some of the experiments are harder than others. Each one has a star rating: the more difficult the experiment is, the more stars it has. We hope you'll try them all.

The Shrinking Arm ★

You will need

a wall

What happens

Your arms seems to shrink. This experiment only takes a minute.

You will have fun trying this on your friends, but first try it out on yourself. Stand and face a wall at arm's length. Hold out your arm in front of you so your fingers just touch the wall. The palm of your hand should face downwards, but this is not important. Keeping your arm straight, slowly swing your arm down and back behind you then swing it forwards again. Do your fingers still reach the wall?

How did it happen? Did your arm really shrink? The answer is very simple. As your arm swings back, the movement makes you sway back slightly. You are still leaning back as your arm moves forward and so your fingers don't reach the wall. Don't worry, your arm is the same length as before.

Ah! But your friends don't know this. Ask them to do this trick and tell them that their arms have shrunk. You'll love their amazement.

Yoo-hoo ★★

You will need

a piece of metal pipe (like scaffolding), about 1m long × 5cm wide
some wire gauze
a gas supply and matches †
scissors
an oven glove or cloth
water
a metal bucket

What happens

You'll have to try this one to find out, but it will only take a few minutes.

Cut out a square piece of wire gauze slightly bigger than the hole in your tube. Push the gauze square into the tube as far as your fingers can reach. There must not be any gaps down the side, so you will need to bend the gauze quite a lot.

Using the oven glove, hold the pipe near the end furthest from the gauze. Hold the pipe upright over a hot gas flame for fifteen to thirty seconds. Keep

† This experiment can be done over a gas ring flame if you are careful, or you could do it at school using a bunsen burner.

your head away from the top of the pipe as the air coming out there is hot enough to burn you. Now move the pipe away from the flame but keep holding it. Within seconds, you should notice something. When you've finished, carefully cool the pipe. Put it in a metal bucket of cold water. It will spit a little, but if you are careful and use a lot of water and don't drop the pipe, this shouldn't be dangerous.

SCAFFOLDING OR METAL TUBE

WIRE GAUZE

GAS →

YOO HOO

When the wire gauze gets hot it vibrates, but it does this so quickly that you cannot see it. This vibration causes the air around the wire to move in waves, just like waves in the sea. The air is also hot, which makes it rise. As these waves of hot air rise up and leave the pipe, they move towards our ears and we hear them – all the sounds we hear are made of air waves. So you have made a wave-making machine. What does the noise remind you of?

The Superhuman Shock Machine ⋆

You will need

> a friend (he or she should wear a jacket)
> a stool
> a small piece of fur or furry fabric (synthetic fur will do)

What happens
This takes three or four minutes. You'll get a shock!

Superman? Wonderwoman? And now we present the superhuman shock machine. You or your friends become charged with electricity and anyone who comes near you will receive an electric shock. Don't worry, the shock is mild.

This experiment works best on a clear, dry day. Ask a friend to stand on a chair and then hit him or her twenty to thirty times on the back of the jacket with the piece of fur. Now put down the fur and hold your fist near your friend's nose. You will receive a slight shock and a spark may jump between the nose and your fist.

How does your friend become a superhuman shock machine? When you strike him the fur transfers tiny, electrically-charged particles called electrons to his jacket. As you continue to hit him he becomes more and more highly charged with electrons. He must stand on a stool or chair because if he stood on the ground the electrons would leave his body and travel to earth. The stool is an insulator, it does not allow electricity to pass through it. As you approach your friend with your fist you discharge him and receive a shock because the electrons pass through your body to earth.

Change positions so that you can become the shock machine. You can try other materials besides fur.

Bending Water   *

You will need

> a water tap
> a plastic ball-point pen
> a woollen jumper

What happens
Abracadabra! Turn your pen into a magic water-wand which attracts the stream of water from your tap. This trick will only take a minute.

Turn on the tap, then carefully turn it down again until you have a very thin stream of water. Rub the pen up and down against your jumper, then hold it very near the water-stream, but make sure it does not touch the water. Move the pen around the top of the stream. What do you see? Your pen becomes a sort of Pied Piper: wherever it goes the water-stream willingly follows.

How does your pen perform this trick? When you rub the pen against your jumper it gains charged particles producing static electricity. The charged pen attracts particles with an opposite charge: it acts like a magnet to the water-stream, which therefore curves towards it.

You can also create a water wand out of a plastic comb. Simply comb your hair and hold the comb near the stream of water. Curly hair is excellent for producing 'electric combs'!

See 'The Superhuman Shock Machine' (page 9) for another experiment involving static electricity.

Dry Water ★

You will need

> a drinking glass
> ground pepper or lycopodium powder
> water

What happens

Dry water! Never! Well, you can dip your finger into a glass of water, and it will keep perfectly dry! It will take you only a minute to make this discovery.

Fill the glass with water and let the water settle. Gently shake ground pepper or lycopodium powder on to the surface of the water until it is completely covered. Make sure the pepper does not sink by keeping the glass absolutely still.

Dip your finger slowly into the water and bring it out again. You will find that your finger is dry, and covered with a fine powder.

How does the powdery substance make the water appear to be dry? On the surface of the water there are invisible particles called molecules. These molecules attract each other by a force and form a 'skin' on the water surface. When you dip your finger into water it normally becomes wet because you break this skin. The grains of pepper or powder help to increase the force which binds these molecules together, and the skin becomes more difficult to break. The floating powder makes the water act like a blown-up balloon. When your finger touches the water surface the skin is not broken, but pushed down. If you press down with sufficient force you will break through the skin and your finger will get wet.

Lycopodium powder is finer than ground pepper but it is not easy to obtain. Ask your science teacher to let you have some.

Tying Yourself in Knots ★

You will need

a piece of stiff cardboard about 18 × 6cm
a piece of string about 60cm long
a nail or something similar to make holes with
a sharp knife or scissors
a stiff plastic or metal ring, such as a curtain
    ring, about 2cm across
a pencil

What happens

In about fifteen minutes you will able to make a puzzle just like the one in the illustration. You start with the ring at one end of the string and the trick is to get it to the other end without bending or breaking anything. It's not as easy as it looks.

Using the nail, make two holes in your card, one in each of the bottom corners, but not too near the corner or the card will tear. The holes should be just big enough for the string to go through. Make a third hole just smaller than the ring, by putting the ring on the centre of the card, drawing around the inside of it and cutting out the hole.

Next, double up the piece of string and pass the loop through the middle hole. Fold the loop down and up under the bottom edge of the card and then thread the two loose ends down through the loop. Tie one end of the string to one of the corner holes. Thread the other end through the metal or plastic ring and then tie this end of the string to the other corner hole. The puzzle should now look like this.

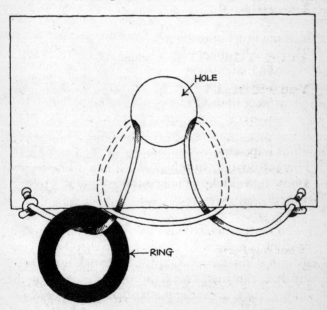

THE DOTTED LINES SHOW THE STRING BEHIND THE CARD

Right. That's the easy bit. Now try and get the ring from one end of the string to the other, but don't lose your temper or tie yourself in knots!

This is the science of topology. People who study it are called topologists. They don't believe in anything being solid, so they invent amazing ways to turn footballs and other things inside out. At first the puzzle looks difficult, but to a topologist it's really very easy. Can you do it? If not, you will find the solution at the back of the book on page 105.

The Bionic Cotton Reel   ★

You will need

- an empty cotton reel
- a small rubber band
- two matchsticks
- adhesive tape
- a piece of candle
- scissors

What happens

The cotton reel stumbles along like a one-legged robot. It will take you a couple of minutes to give the reel a life of its own.

Use a matchstick to push the rubber band through the central hole of the cotton reel so that it sticks out at both ends (fig 1). Snap a matchstick in two and slip half the matchstick through one loop of the rubber band. Tape the matchstick and rubber band to the reel (fig 2).

Cut off about a centimetre of candle and poke out

the wick with the scissors leaving a hole through the centre. Push the free loop of the rubber band through the candle (fig 3). Take a whole matchstick and place it snugly through this loop (fig 4). Wind up the matchstick then place the cotton reel on a smooth surface. It will click-clack along like a small robot.

The experiment shows the same principle as that used in the old clockwork train sets (if you haven't seen one ask your Dad or Mum about them), where a spring is used rather than a rubber band. When you wind up the matchstick, you store up energy in the rubber band. The more you coil the band, the greater the energy it will release on unwinding, and the further the bionic cotton reel will run. See how far it can go on its own.

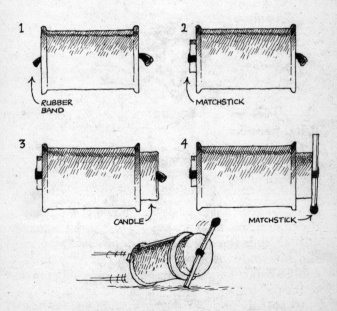

Help! I'm Taking Off! ★

You will need

a doorway

What happens
You will not actually be able to fly, but you will know how it feels just before take-off. It will only take a minute.

Stand in an open doorway between the doorposts, and place the back of your right hand against one doorpost and the back of your left hand against the other without bending your elbows. Press your

hands as hard as you possibly can against the doorposts, and count slowly to thirty while you do this.
When you reach thirty, allow your arms to relax by
your side, and walk forward two or three paces
from the door. In a few seconds something very
funny will happen. Your arms will float upwards
and you will feel like a human bird.

Why do your arms begin to feel like wings? When
you push out against the doorposts you are really
trying to make them move, but you do not succeed
– I hope. As you press outwards, a high tension is
built up in the muscles that move your arms; when
you move away you remove the cause of the tension
in your muscles. Your arms relax, and they swing
upwards as a result. Happy flying!

Will You Make a Good Test-pilot? ★★

You will need

    a 12-inch (30–cm) ruler
    paper
    adhesive tape
    scissors
    felt-tip pen
    a friend

What happens
Test-pilots must have very sharp reflexes. You can
make an instrument that tests these reflexes, and it
takes only a few minutes.

Tightly wrap a long sheet of paper around the ruler,
cut it to size, and tape the ends down neatly. Divide

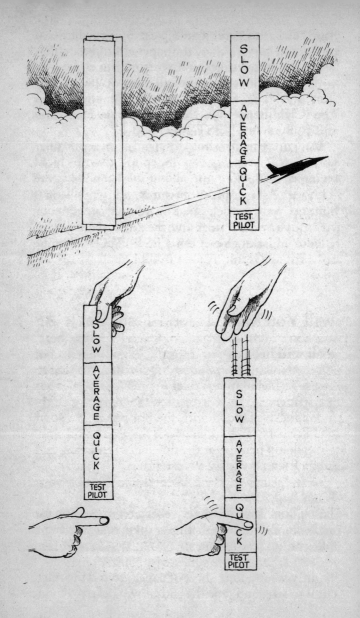

your ruler into three equal parts by drawing two lines across the width of the paper around the ruler. Draw another line about 1cm from the end of the ruler. Label your ruler by writing 'SLOW' in the top third, 'AVERAGE' in the middle third, and 'QUICK' in the last third. In the space below 'QUICK', write 'TEST-PILOT'.

Ask your friend to hold his hand open so the ruler can pass between his forefinger and thumb. Hold the ruler longways just above his hand with the 'TEST-PILOT' section nearest to it. Without warning, let the ruler fall. The point at which your friend catches the ruler indicates the speed of his reflexes. If he catches it on 'TEST-PILOT' then he has extremely fast reactions, but if he snaps his fingers before the ruler falls he is disqualified. If he misses the ruler altogether he will not make a good test-pilot unless he practises hard.

A reflex is an involuntary response, that is, one you don't think about, to something you see, hear, smell, taste or feel. For example, if you touch a hot poker you whip away your hand without saying to yourself: 'Shall I remove my hand?' A test-pilot has fast reflexes because he must respond very quickly to danger, as you do with the hot poker. As soon as you see the ruler move, your fingers should close to catch it. The shorter the time between seeing and catching, the faster are your reflexes.

Swap places and ask your friend to test your reflexes now.

You can design your own reflex tester; for instance, football fans might like one with the fastest area labelled TOP GOALIE. Remember, you can improve your reflexes by constant practice.

The Fizzy Lemonade Factory ★★

You will need

a lemon *or* some citric acid
bicarbonate of soda
sugar
a teaspoon
a drinking glass
a clean empty bottle with a tight-fitting cap

What happens

You produce lots of fizzing lemonade to your own taste. It takes only a few minutes to make a glass of lemonade, but longer if you want to make enough for all your friends.

Squeeze the juice from the lemon into the drinking glass *or* place a teaspoon of citric acid into the glass. (Lemon juice contains citric acid and water). Add water until the glass is half-full and stir, if necessary, to dissolve any solid citric acid. Stir in half a teaspoon of bicarbonate of soda, and you have lemonade which sparkles, pops and fizzes. Don't taste it yet; it will be very sour. Add some sugar and stir until the taste is to your liking.

You will notice that the fizz soon disappears. A gas, called carbon dioxide, causes the bubbling, and if the lemonade is exposed to the air, the gas escapes and the fizzing stops. The gas is released by a chemical reaction between the bicarbonate of soda and the citric acid. The fizzing stops when these two have finished reacting. You can overcome this problem by making the lemonade in a bottle. Use lemon juice, or citric acid and water, as before, then add some sugar. Shake the bottle gently to dissolve the sugar, add the bicarbonate of soda, then top up the bottle with water. Screw on the cap and you can drink the sparkling lemonade at your leisure.

You can change the amount of the various ingredients, but once you know how much sugar you like, add it before you add the bicarbonate of soda and the rest of the water, then you will have a nice fresh fizz. You'll become very popular with your friends.

House Phone ★★

You will need

> two empty tin cans
> about 10m of thin wire (thin string could be used instead)
> two buttons
> a small tack
> a small hammer

What happens

You can talk or whisper to a friend at the other end of your house and he will hear you perfectly. It will take about ten minutes to make this house phone.

The lids of the tin cans should be removed carefully to make sure that no sharp edges are left. Use the hammer and tack to make a small hole in the bottom of each tin can. Thread one end of the wire into one of the cans through the hole you have just made, then thread it through one of the buttons. Tie a small knot in the wire to prevent the button slipping off. Join the other end of the wire to the other tin can in the same way. When you pull the two cans as far apart from each other as possible the wire should stretch between them with the buttons securing the ends of the wire inside the cans.

You have now made your house phone. You can use the tin cans as mouth-pieces and ear-pieces to have a conversation with a friend, as long as you keep the wire taut. *Don't pull the wire with a sudden jerk.* It could snap back into your face.

People, animals and objects create sounds as a result of vibrations. These cause sound waves to travel through air or other substances. The vocal chords of humans vibrate and send out sound waves. When you talk or make a sound into the tin can the button vibrates and sends sound waves along the wire to the other tin can. There the other button vibrates and sends reflected sound waves through the tin can to the other person's ear. Sound travels much faster along solids, such as wire, than it does through air, so the house phone is an efficient way of sending messages.

You can use thin string instead of wire, though it's not quite as good. Remember that it's difficult to see wire, so be careful not to use the house phone where you might trip someone up.

The Shaky Hand Game ★★★

You will need

  a shoe-box with lid
  a thin wire clothes hanger
  1.5V battery
  fuse wire
  insulating tape
  scissors
  1.5V M.E.S. light bulb†
  M.E.S. bulb holder for the above bulb†

What happens

You will make a piece of equipment that will test your nerves; a light will come on when your hand shakes. This game should take you about twenty minutes to put together, and you'll have great fun with your friends seeing whose hand is the steadiest.

Tape the battery securely to the inside of the shoe-box at one end (fig 1). Then use the scissors to make a small hole in the lid of the shoe-box, directly above the battery. Cut off a piece of fuse wire long enough to reach from the top of the battery through the hole and extend 1 to 2 centimetres beyond the

† These are small screw-fittings.

23

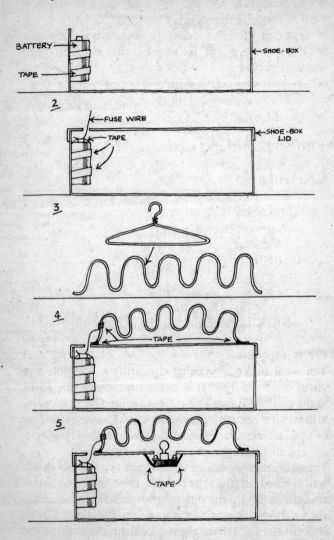

1. BATTERY — TAPE — SHOE-BOX

2. FUSE WIRE — TAPE — SHOE-BOX LID

3.

4. TAPE

5. TAPE

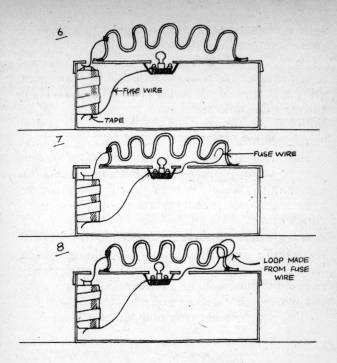

hole (fig 2). Tape one end of the wire to the cap of the battery. Unwind the clothes hanger so it is almost straight, then bend it into a series of U-shaped curves (fig 3). Tape one end of this thick wire to the lid of the shoe-box near the fuse wire, and tape the other end, securely, to the opposite end of the lid. Use the insulating tape to bind the end of the fuse wire to the wiggly wire (fig 4).

Cut a larger hole in the centre of the shoe-box lid. Screw the bulb into the holder, raise the lid slightly, and push the bulb up through the hole from under the lid. Tape the bulb-holder to the lid (fig 5). Cut a length of fuse wire to run from the bottom of the battery to the bulb-holder. Tape one end of the fuse wire to the base of the battery and fix the other end in the screw of the bulb–holder (fig 6).

Pierce a small hole in the lid of the shoe-box near the other screw of the bulb–holder. Cut about 30 centimetres of fuse wire, thread one end down through this hole and secure it in the screw of the bulb–holder (fig 7). Bend the free end of the fuse wire round the thick wire and fasten it into a loop with a diameter of about 3 centimetres (fig 8). Test out the width of the loop by running it along the length of the wiggly wire. You will notice that the bulb lights up whenever the two wires make contact.

If you can run the looped wire along the length of the wiggly wire without the bulb lighting up you have a steady hand, but you will almost certainly need some practice before you can do this. When the two wires make contact you complete an electrical circuit, which makes your bulb light up. Have fun!

Grow Your Own Spaghetti! ★★★★

You will need

> 1 packet of 'Vegetable spaghetti' seeds
> a small space in a garden, or a small box full of soil, or a 'grow bag'

What happens
The fruit produced by the plants is related to the marrow. If picked when ripe and cooked properly the result is a vegetable very similar to spaghetti. The seeds take up to ten weeks to grow and produce fruit. The fruit take ten to twenty minutes to cook.

Buy some seeds from a good seed supplier or garden shop. Full instructions for planting should appear on the packet. Make sure you plant the seeds just below the soil surface, allowing at least 200 cubic centimetres of soil for each plant. It is a good idea to plant several seeds in each plant's section of soil and then pull out the weakest seedlings when they start growing. Grow the plants outdoors during the spring and summer.

To cook the vegetable, boil it for ten to twenty minutes in water. Experiment until you get the cooking time exactly right so that when you cut open the cooked marrow it is full of spaghetti-like strands. You may need to separate out the strands a little with a fork. They taste nice just with a little salt and butter, or you can add a spaghetti sauce, cheese, or whatever you like.

Of course this isn't real spaghetti. Real spaghetti is man-made from flour and water, and although most people think it's from Italy, it was actually discovered in China by Marco Polo who brought it to Italy.

The vegetable spaghetti is a type of marrow. There are lots of other plants related to marrows, including cucumbers, squashes and pumpkins. Your vegetable only looks like spaghetti because of the way it is cooked. If you cook it for too long it goes very squashy and if you don't cook it enough it stays hard. If it doesn't work first time, try again. Very few people even know about 'vegetable spaghetti' so it is worth trying until you get it right. Then try telling your teachers you have grown spaghetti, and see their reaction!

Follow That Ant ★

You will need

> a big lid from a large tin
> a small lid
> water
> 2 flat ice-lolly sticks or 2 straws (flattened)
> honey (or very sweet water)
> glue or plasticine (if available)
> a place where you can find ants

What happens

You will learn how ants know where to find food. It doesn't take long to set up, but remember it can only be done when ants are to be found, i.e. spring, summer and early autumn.

If you have some glue or plasticine, stick the small lid inside the big lid, otherwise just place the small lid in the middle of the big lid and hold it in position. Find a place where there are ants, but not right next to an ants' nest or you might get covered in them. Don't use red ants, they bite. When you've found some ants put the two lids down near them. Pour water into the big lid to form a moat, then pour the honey (or sweet water) into the small lid. Now put one of the ice-lolly sticks down so that one end is on the ground near the ants and the other end is resting on the small lid with the honey. The stick must not touch the big lid. Put the other stick down so that one end is on the ground and the other end touches the rim of the large lid.

Now watch. After a while the ants will find the lids and the two bridges. At first they will walk up both bridges but when some ants find the honey that should change. You should see that after some

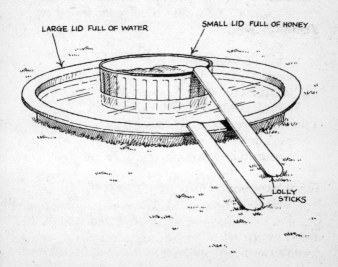

LARGE LID FULL OF WATER

SMALL LID FULL OF HONEY

LOLLY STICKS

of the ants have eaten some honey and gone back to their nest, most of the ants then come straight back to the honey. Keep watching until this happens. When it does, change the sticks round. Move the honey one so that it only touches the big lid and make the other bridge only touch the lid with the honey. Now all the ants should go to the water.

Why does this happen? Well, ants are able to communicate with each other in several ways. One way is to leave a scent trail wherever they go. In this case, when an ant finds honey, it marks the way back to the nest with a smelly liquid. Most of the ants find the smell and follow it. When they find honey they collect some and return home, also leaving a smelly trail, so the path to the honey gets smellier and smellier. If you swop the bridges over, the ants end up at the water, not the honey, because they continue to follow the trail.

Most animals use their sense of smell a lot. In fact, humans are unusual among animals for relying on smell so little. You can't track your friend by his smell, can you?

Musical Straws ★★

You will need

about 10 drinking straws
scissors
a piece of stiff card (say 30 × 15cm)
adhesive tape

What happens
You can make a mouth organ in about ten minutes.

Flatten about one centimetre of one end of a drinking straw. Cut each side of this flat end so that you have a point (fig 1). Moisten the pointed flaps with your tongue then blow through them. It may take a little practice but you will soon obtain a musical note which you can vary slightly if you blow harder or softer. You have made a very simple instrument operating on a similar principle to that of ancient reed pipes.

Cut about 2 centimetres off the opposite end of the straw and blow again. What do you notice? Cut off another 2 centimetres and blow; the pitch becomes higher as the straw gets shorter.

Sound consists of vibrations, and in the case of the musical straw, blowing on the pointed flaps makes the air inside the straw vibrate. There is a certain point at which the air inside the straw will most easily vibrate and this corresponds to the 'natural frequency' of the straw. The shorter the straw, the higher the natural frequency, and the higher the note. When playing a recorder you regulate the length of tubing in which the air can vibrate by stopping or opening holes along the length of the recorder. For low notes you increase the length, for higher notes you allow a relatively short length. The same principle operates in the mouth organ.

Now you can make a very primitive mouth organ, but it will be a matter of trial-and-error to reach a proper scale. Take the scale doh-ray-me-fah-soh-lah-te-doh. Use a long straw for the low doh, then try various shorter lengths for the next straw until you reach a ray, and so on up the scale. If you don't want all the bother of making a perfect scale, take ten straws and make flaps at the end of each one. Use these to make a series of straws from full length to very small, and line them up from the shortest to the longest. Tape them to the stiff card in this order (fig 2). There should be about 2 centimetres between each straw and the blowing ends should be level.

When you have made your mouth organ take care not to annoy or scare your neighbours because some of the notes from the straw pipes are truly dreadful. You should be able to play a version of any tune with practice, but don't expect to become a musical genius.

See the 'Yoo-hoo' experiment on page 7 for a strange musical pipe.

Make Your Own Breakfast ★

You will need

    a saucepan or frying pan with a lid
    a cup of uncooked rice
    a gas or electric cooker
    a little oil or butter
    milk
    a bowl and a spoon

What happens

After about five minutes you will have made a breakfast which you can eat hot or cold.

To begin, put about a teaspoonful of oil or butter in the pan. Heat the pan but do not let the oil or butter smoke or burn. Add the rice after a couple of minutes and put the lid on straight away.

After a minute or so you will hear popping sounds. From now on you should shake the pan gently while it heats. The air inside the grains of rice is being heated and so it is expanding. Eventually it expands enough to explode the rice. The noise you hear is the rice popping just like pop-corn. After about three minutes take the pan away from the heat. Carefully open it and see if all the rice has popped. It looks whiter when it has. If you think it's finished pour it out into the bowl.

If you want to eat the rice hot, just add milk, and some sugar if you like, and there you are. If not, leave it to cool and then add milk and sugar. For a different recipe, try it Chinese style. Pop some rice in the same way and then pour sweet and sour sauce on it.

The Radish Flower ★★

You will need

a radish
a paring knife (small, sharp vegetable knife)
a glass of water, preferably iced

What happens

You will learn an ancient Chinese art and find out
that some things are more scientific than you think.
It takes about an hour to work.

When we were at school most boys used to think
learning to cook was something girls did and science
was for boys. Not true. Cooking is a science for
both girls and boys. To cook well you must follow
the rules and if you do you can usually predict what
will happen. That makes cookery a science and
nowadays it is called domestic science in schools.

By experimenting with food we can also find
things out. Begin by cutting off the top and bottom
of your radish, but only cut off a small amount.
Stand the radish up on the larger flat end. Next
make two cuts at right angles down into the radish;
each cut must go through the top and must not
go more than three-quarters of the way down the
length (fig 1). Now cut the radish in a circle, straight
down but again do not cut down more than you did
for the other cuts (fig 2).

So far the radish should still be in one piece. If any
section falls out, try another radish. When you
finish cutting, drop the radish in a glass of water. If
you want to use the radish later for decorating food
try to use iced water. Leave the radish for an hour
and then take it out to see what has happened. With

luck, you will find that it has opened up like a flower. You can use these 'flowers' to decorate food and, of course, they can be eaten too.

Why is this scientific? Well, we need science to explain what has happened. Obviously the cut pieces of the radish have moved and, as with all plants, this only happens for one of two reasons. Either the plant has grown, or extra water has been absorbed into the plant tissue and caused the movement. In the case of the radish you can probably guess that water was the cause. The radish, like all parts of plants, is made up of lots of 'living bricks' called cells. These are full of all the chemicals a plant needs to live, most of which are dissolved in water. So you can imagine that the liquid inside a cell is a bit like a strong drink or soup.

Outside the plant cells of your radish there is just ordinary water in a glass. When you leave the radish, the water in the glass passes into the plant cells and weakens the soupy mixture. Water will always be drawn like this into a very strong mixture, as long as the strong mixture is separated from the water by a special layer of tissue which only allows weak solutions or water to pass through it. The walls of plant cells have a layer of this special tissue, so the cells of the radish allow the water to pass in but they will not allow the soupy mixture to pass out. In the science of biology this type of movement is very important in plants and animals and it has the special name of osmosis.

Now, to understand why the cut sections of the radish move apart, imagine two rubber boxes full of water stuck side by side (fig 3). If you pump more water into box 2, what will happen? It will get bigger but because it is stuck to box 1 it will only be able to expand on its free side and so the boxes will

1   SIDE VIEW OF CUT RADISH

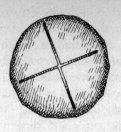

TOP VIEW OF CUT RADISH

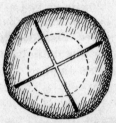

2   CUT THE RADISH ONCE MORE
     IN A CIRCLE IN THE POSITION
     SHOWN BY THE DOTTED LINE

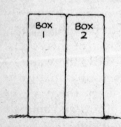

3   RUBBER BOXES
     FILLED WITH WATER

4   THIS IS WHAT HAPPENS IF
     YOU PUMP EXTRA WATER
     INTO BOX 2

bend to look like those illustrated in fig 4.

In the radish, the cells on the outside, coloured red, do not allow much water in. All the white cells allow water to pass in freely so it is just like the situation in the boxes. The sections of the radish will bend and that is why it opens up like the petals of a flower.

But what has all this got to do with Chinese art? As you probably know the Chinese invented or discovered lots of things, and these included the art of cutting vegetables and meat. They can make food look like almost anything and have special schools to teach people how to do this. Now you, too, can make a radish flower. You may be able to think up all sorts of different things to make from other vegetables like carrots, tomatoes or cucumbers, just as the Chinese have for hundreds of years.

A Plant That Eats Animals! ★★★

You will need

a 5-in (125-mm) diameter dwarf pot
a 'Venus fly trap' plant
some sand and moss peat
rain-water
a saucer or plant 'tray' about 15cm wide
a small paintbrush

What happens

You will grow a plant that moves very quickly. It can catch its own food and will eat while you watch it!

This experiment can take quite a long time but if you have patience everybody you show this to will enjoy it. Start it in spring or summer.

First you must get everything ready for your plant. Find or buy a 4- or 5-inch (105- or 125-mm) plant pot. Make sure it is a 'dwarf' pot, that is, a short pot which needs less earth. Soft plastic pots are best as they are difficult to break. Also find or buy a plant saucer to stand the pot in. It should have sides about 2 centimetres high and it should be about 2 centimetres wider than the pot. Unless you know a gardener you will also need to buy sand and moss peat but you will be able to use what is left over for other experiments. Mix a small amount of sand with about twice as much moss peat. You should make enough to almost fill the pot.

If you buy a mature plant you will not have the problem of waiting for it to grow and you can experiment straight away. (Look in the back of the book for a place where you can buy good plants.) The plant will probably arrive in a small pot. If it does, replant it in the pot which you have already prepared for it. It likes warmth and sun and will be quite happy on a warm window-sill. Always use rain-water if possible, or else tap water that you have boiled first and allowed to cool. If you water the plant with ordinary tap water it will die.

Once you have your plant you can begin. It should have traps on the ends of the leaves and they should be about 1 centimetre or more in length. Choose one which is fully open and tickle inside it with the paintbrush. What happens? Before you hurry to try this again, read on. Look inside another trap and you will see that each half has three very small 'hairs'. But these aren't really hairs. They are triggers. Now very carefully touch one of these triggers just *once*. Nothing happens. Try touching it three or four times. The trap should close. Don't touch the plant any more or you may damage it. Leave it to close or open by itself.

Why do the traps close, you will be asking. Well, the two halves of the trap close to catch insects such as flies. The Venus fly trap is a carnivorous (meat-eating) or insectivorous (insect-eating) plant. It catches flies because it grows naturally in swamps where there is no real soil so it cannot absorb essential minerals through its roots. The triggers sense when an insect is inside and the trap snaps shut. As you saw, a trigger doesn't close the trap unless it is tickled a lot, so even the rain will not shut the trap.

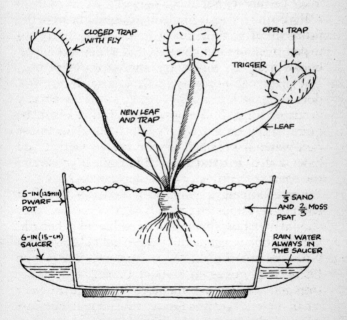

Once the trap is shut the plant digests the food just as you do in your stomach. It uses chemicals called enzymes which break down the food so that it can be absorbed by the plant. When a trap opens again after an insect has been digested, you will see the undigested body shell of the insect left inside – all that remains to prove the insect was there!

How the trap actually shuts is rather complicated. In some way the movement of water is able to make it open and close. You will have seen that water passes through the cells of plants and causes the plant tissue to move in the previous experiment, 'The Radish Flower', but the Venus fly trap is special in that the two halves of the trap move so quickly. Look after your plant and you can surprise your friends with it about once every two or three weeks. If you feed it more often and all the traps get full at the same time, the plant might die. It can live in soil without eating insects, if you keep it watered, so it will survive the winter without any flies.

Counting Up To 1000 On Your Fingers! ★★★

You will need

10 fingers, or 10 of anything like buttons, straws, etc

What happens

Most people can count to ten on their fingers. Some can even count a little higher but you will learn how to count up to 1023 on just ten fingers.

Start with both palms facing you but fingers and thumbs down (ie your hands closed into fists). If you put your right thumb up that means '1'. For '2' put your right index finger up and the right thumb down. For '3', both your right thumb and right index finger should be up. Now if a finger is up we can call it a '1'. If a finger is down we can call it a '0'. So if you have ten fingers, nought in finger counting is

	0	0	0	0	0	0	0	0	0	0
1 is	0	0	0	0	0	0	0	0	0	1
2 is	0	0	0	0	0	0	0	0	1	0
3 is	0	0	0	0	0	0	0	0	1	1

Can you see what 4 would be? The answer is

	0	0	0	0	0	0	0	1	0	0
5 is	0	0	0	0	0	0	0	1	0	1
6 is	0	0	0	0	0	0	0	1	1	0
7 is	0	0	0	0	0	0	0	1	1	1
8 is	0	0	0	0	0	0	1	0	0	0

You should be able to work out the rest for yourself. Notice that you can count up to 15 on only four fingers!

This type of counting is called binary. It means there are only 2 numbers, 0 and 1. It is the type of mathematics used by computers.

Now you should be able to carry on for yourself and count up to 1023. To help you check if you are doing it correctly two more numbers are given below.

32 is	0	0	0	0	1	0	0	0	0	0
167 is	0	0	1	0	1	0	0	1	1	1

See the illustration overleaf.

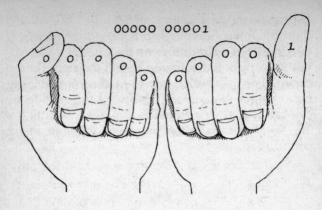

00000 00001

1 THIS POSITION REPRESENTS ONE OR BINARY 00000 00001

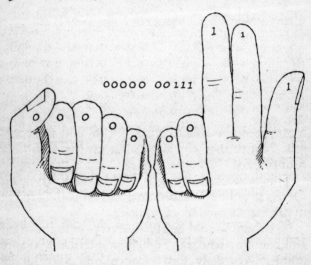

00000 00111

2 THIS POSITION REPRESENTS SEVEN OR BINARY 00000 00111

Flame-proof Paper   ★★★

You will need

    a square of brown parcel paper (22cm × 22cm)
    8 paper clips
    water
    a candle
    matches
    an empty tin can (the size of a soft-drink can)
    a hammer
    a large nail

What happens

In ten to fifteen minutes you will manage to use the paper as a saucepan in which to boil water. Strangely, the flame will not burn the paper. Make sure there is an adult present when you use the matches or a flame.

Put the square piece of paper on a table with its shiny side uppermost. Fold up each side so that it is about 4 centimetres high (fig 1). Fold each corner along a side and secure it with two paper clips (fig 2). Test your paper saucepan to make sure it can hold a little water.

    Make sure that the top of the can has been removed completely, leaving no sharp edges, then using the hammer and nail, carefully punch holes in the side of the can. About ten holes will do but make sure some are very near the bottom. Light the candle and let some wax drop into the bottom of the can. Blow out the candle and quickly stick it to the soft wax in the can. You now have a home-made heater (fig 3).

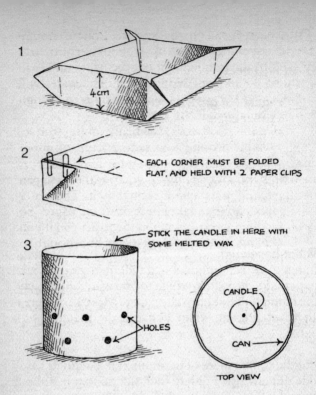

1

4 cm

2

EACH CORNER MUST BE FOLDED
FLAT, AND HELD WITH 2 PAPER CLIPS

3

STICK THE CANDLE IN HERE WITH
SOME MELTED WAX

HOLES

CANDLE

CAN

TOP VIEW

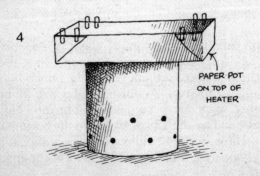

4

PAPER POT
ON TOP OF
HEATER

Put the paper pan on a flat surface. Pour in enough water to cover the bottom up to about 2 centimetres deep. Light the candle, then put the paper saucepan on top of the tin can. Now watch. The water will soon boil but the paper will not burn even though the flame can touch it (fig 4).

The reason this works is really quite simple. Water boils at a quite low temperature of about 100°C but paper will only burn if the temperature is much higher than that. When you put the saucepan over the flame, the paper is heated by it. The water in the paper pan then takes heat from the paper. So as long as there is some water in the paper pan it will take heat out of the paper until it gets hot enough to boil. This stops the paper from getting very hot. In fact, the paper could only reach 100°C after all the water had boiled away. Then it would quickly catch fire. Don't let this happen. Remove the paper saucepan from the heat as soon as the water starts to boil.

Square Eggs ★

You will need

> a little edible oil, butter or margarine
> one or more small or medium eggs
> a plastic box (see below)
> a saucepan and some water
> a gas or electric ring
> a refrigerator
> a spoon
> a knife
> string, or a heavy object

What happens
In twenty-five minutes you will be able to serve someone a cooked egg. However, instead of the normal shape this egg will be square.

First find a plastic box which measures about 4cm × 4cm × 4cm. A good place to look for one is a toy shop. If it sells the kind of small plastic boxes with games inside, such as the one where you have to roll little balls around into special holes, you can buy one and very carefully use a knife to take off one side and empty out all the bits. You'll find the box is useful in another experiment, 'Square Tomatoes' (page 57), so look after it.

Put some water in the saucepan and carefully add the egg. The water should just cover it. Now heat the water and let it boil for ten to twelve minutes. Meanwhile grease the inside of the plastic box using a very little amount of cooking oil, butter or margarine. If you are using the kind of games box described above, remember to grease the piece from the open side as well.

When the ten to twelve minutes have passed, switch off the heat and take out the egg with the spoon. Save the hot water. Carefully and patiently crack and remove the egg shell without damaging the egg. This is quite difficult because the egg is very hot so do only a little bit at a time. Do not let the egg cool down too much. If necessary put it back in the hot water for a few seconds.

When you have taken off all the shell, wash the egg in the hot water, shake off the water and put the egg into the plastic box, pointed end first. Do not push too hard. Gently ease it in, poking the sides with your finger if necessary. Finally, put the lid on the box and place it in the refrigerator. You will

need to put something heavy on the lid to hold it closed, or else you can tie down the lid with string. Leave the egg in the cold until you want it, but wait for at least fifteen minutes. When you tip the egg out it will stay the shape of the box.

Before we see why this has happened let's make one or two things clear. First, the egg isn't square at all. A square is completely flat, so obviously the egg can't be square. Instead we call it cubic because, unlike a square which has a width and a length, our cube has width, length and height as well. Now, what shape was the ordinary cooked egg (in its shell)? It wasn't square or cubic or even round. Believe it or not, that strange shape has an even stranger name. It's called an oblate spheroid! This is not as useless a piece of information as you may think. Next time a teacher asks you what is the shape of our planet earth you can tell him or her it's an oblate spheroid – because, in fact, the earth is egg-shaped.

But why did the egg become cubic? The egg is made from lots of chemicals which are almost all joined together. When the egg is raw they are only loosely joined or bonded together but, by cooking the egg, we make the bonds stronger. Chemicals which are only weakly bonded together are liquids. Strong bonds make solids. So the cooking caused a chemical reaction in which the egg changed from a liquid to a solid. The box acted as a mould instead of the egg shell, but we could have used a container of any shape. While the egg was hot, the bonds were still a little weak but the refrigerator allowed the egg to 'set'.

Smelly Stuff   ★

You will need

for perfumed water
rain-water
½-litre container
½-litre bottle with
  screw top lid
fresh flower petals

for perfumed oil
baby oil
clean cotton cloth
small bottle with lid
greaseproof paper
fresh flower petals
2 saucers
a weight

What happens
The very first scientists were people who learnt how to use plants to make drinks, medicines, dyes and

many other things. Now, with just a few minutes' work, you can make perfume the way they did hundreds or maybe thousands of years ago.

To make *perfumed water* first collect your fresh rain-water and flower petals. You will need at least ten large flowers such as roses or three tablespoons of small flowers such as lavender. Make sure the flower you choose has a pleasant smell. It is best to use only one type of flower at a time. Put the petals only in your ½-litre container and cover them with rain-water. Leave this jar covered. After about three days pour the scented water out and throw away the petals. Put more petals in the water if you can get some. If possible, add new petals three or four times. You can then use the scented water as per-fume. Use it quickly as the scent may not last long. Store it in a screw-top bottle.

To make a *perfumed oil*, first cut out squares of cotton cloth. Each square should just fit on your saucer. Pour some baby oil into one of the saucers, ready to soak each piece of cloth in as you need it. Also have ready the petals of a nicely scented flower. On the second saucer you can now make a large pile of alternate layers of cotton soaked in oil and petals. It will be like an enormous cotton cloth and petal sandwich. When you have finished, cover the pile with a piece of greaseproof paper and put a large weight on it. Leave the pile for about three days. If you have more petals take the pile apart after this time and throw away the old ones, then use the new ones to make a fresh pile with the same oil-soaked cloth. When you have no more petals throw all the old ones away. Now use clean hands to squeeze as much oil as you can out of the cloth squares into a saucer and then pour the oil into a bottle. You have made a perfumed oil to use or give away.

You made a perfume by removing, or extracting, the smell from the flower petals. The smell is naturally found in oils made by the flower. When you make the perfumed water see if you can find any tiny drops of oil on the water surface. These are where most of the smell will be and these little drops are very precious. They are called 'otto' or 'attar'.

Attar of roses was well known even to the ancient Egyptians, so perfume-making really is a very old science. In fact, flowers were probably the first things used in trying to cure people of diseases so you may be performing some of the very first experiments in medicine. Modern perfume-making uses flowers, beetles and animal fats.

Beaten By a Matchbox   ★

You will need

> a friend
> an empty matchbox
> a thick carpet

What happens
You will discover, to your surprise, that you cannot do a perfectly simple trick. It will take you two minutes.

Kneel down with your knees together, placing your arms on the carpet directly in front of you with your elbows touching your knees (fig 1). Put your hands together, palm to palm, and point your fingers. Ask your friend to place a matchbox on the carpet at the

1

2

3

4

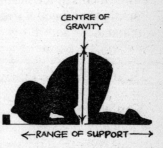

CENTRE OF
GRAVITY

←RANGE OF SUPPORT→

5

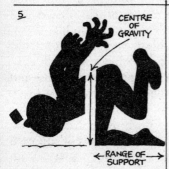

CENTRE
OF
GRAVITY

←RANGE OF
SUPPORT→

tips of your fingers. In this position you will find that you can grasp the matchbox between your teeth without using your hands (fig 2). But don't pick it up yet. Sit up without moving your legs and place your hands behind your back (fig 3). Lower your head and pick up the matchbox between your teeth without using your hands. Can you do this without falling over?

If you pick up the matchbox then give yourself a pat on the back – if you can. The reason you find it difficult or impossible to pick up the matchbox is because of your centre of gravity. Gravity is the force that prevents people floating up to space. Gravity acts downwards upon every point of your body, but there is a point about which these forces are balanced and this is called the centre of gravity. We will encounter it again in the 'It Rolls Uphill' experiment on page 66. Its position depends upon the size and shape of your body. If you are tall and skinny with an enormous head, your centre of gravity will be high, but if you are short and stocky it will be low down. Generally, the centre of gravity is somewhere in the small of your back. When the centre of gravity of an object is low down and directly above its point of support it is stable. When the centre of gravity is high, and displaced from above its point of support, the object is unstable. In the first part of this experiment both your arms and legs support you and a vertical line drawn down from your centre of gravity will fall within this range of support (fig 4). With your arms behind your back, your legs are the only means of support. As you bend over, your centre of gravity is no longer directly above any point of support and you become unstable and topple over (fig 5).

Examples of centre of gravity and stability are

reflected in nature. Tortoises have a low centre of gravity, well within their range of support, so it is very difficult to knock them over. Babies have a large head relative to the rest of their body; their centre of gravity is high making them a little unstable and so nature makes them compensate by crawling and spreading their weight over a large area to give a greater range of support.

Always try the matchbox trick on a thick carpet otherwise you may get a nasty bump on the nose.

It's Alive! ★★★

You will need

> very clean hands!
> ½ litre of orange peel (3 mugs full)
> 3 litres of boiling water
> campden tablets
> a large plastic box or bucket to hold the peel and water
> a large glass or plastic bottle (to hold almost 4 litres or 1 gallon)
> a small piece of fresh root ginger if available (about 10g or ¼ oz)
> 230g (about ½ lb) sultanas
> 1.25kg (about 3 lbs) sugar
> a teaspoon of dried yeast (not bakers' yeast)
> nutrient and activator if available
> a fermentation lock with rubber bung or cotton wool
> a small mixing bowl
> a small knife
> a spoon

What happens

This experiment shows you how to make your own wine. It takes about four to six weeks but you only need to do a small amount of work. You will need to spend up to twenty minutes about four times during the six weeks.

Collect the peel every time you eat an orange. Scrape off all the white pith and cut the peel into very thin strips (called julienne strips in domestic science). Store the strips in a closed tin or plastic box until you have enough.

When you are ready, put all your peel into the large plastic box or bucket. It must be very clean. (In fact everything you use must be as clean as possible. It is best to use very hot water to sterilise everything before you use it, so ask an adult to do this for you. Remember, hot water can be very dangerous.) Pour 3 litres of boiling water on the peel. Then drop in one campden tablet. (You can buy these and all the other things you need for this experiment from a shop which specialises in home-made wine. See the Useful Addresses list in the back of the book.) Cover the box or bucket with a lid or a clean cloth and leave it for four days.

Take out the orange peel and throw it away. Pour the remaining orange-water into a large bottle. Add about 10 grams of fresh root ginger if it is available. Also add the sterilised sultanas, 1 kilogram of sugar and the teaspoon of dried yeast. You may also add nutrient and activator if you have bought them. The instructions will come with these. Finally add some more water, which you have boiled and allowed to cool, until the bottle is almost full. Now put the fermentation lock in the bung and fit this to the bottle. If you didn't buy one of these, fit a plug made

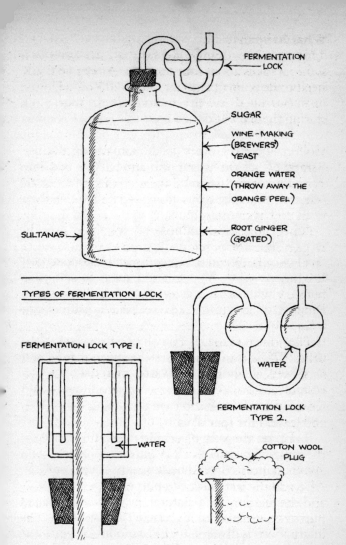

FERMENTATION LOCK

SUGAR

WINE-MAKING
(BREWERS')
YEAST

ORANGE WATER
(THROW AWAY THE
ORANGE PEEL)

ROOT GINGER
(GRATED)

SULTANAS →

TYPES OF FERMENTATION LOCK

FERMENTATION LOCK TYPE 1.

WATER

WATER

FERMENTATION LOCK
TYPE 2.

COTTON WOOL
PLUG

of cotton wool instead (see illustration page 55).

You can now leave the mixture in a warm place and look at it from time to time. After one week unplug the bottle, pour out some of the liquid into a small bowl and add about 120 grams of sugar. Stir until it dissolves and then pour this liquid back into the bottle. Put the fermentation lock or cotton wool back in. Ten days later do the same again but use only 60 grams of sugar this time. Also add one campden tablet this time.

Now wait about one more week. By this time you will have noticed bubbles in the liquid. During the time the liquid is in the bottle it bubbles quickly at first and then gradually more slowly until it finally stops. When it has completely stopped you have made wine. You can add sugar to suit your taste. A wine with a sweet taste is called a sweet wine. A wine without a sweet taste is called a dry wine.

The wine is made by a tiny living organism called yeast. While it grows it uses the sugar as food and produces alcohol as a waste material. Carbon dioxide gas is also produced as waste and you could see this as the tiny bubbles in the young wine. This process has the special name of fermentation. Yeast is found on the skin of uncultivated fruit but your yeast was a special one. It is better for making wine than uncultivated yeast because it has been carefully grown and selected for this purpose.

Fermentation is a natural process which man probably discovered by accident. When wine is made there is always a small amount of yeast left floating in the liquid so all wine is actually alive. We eat lots of 'live' food. Yogurt (and cheese) can be 'live' – see the 'Living Food' experiment, page 83. Vinegar can also contain living organisms as you will see in 'Germs', on page 82. If you intend to use your wine to try the 'Germs' experiment or if you want to store it for drinking later, you should filter off the sediment and sultanas before storing it in closed bottles. The wine should then last for up to a year if no one drinks it first!

Square Tomatoes ★★★

You will need

- 1 packet of tomato seeds or the seeds from a fresh tomato
- a small space in a garden, small box full of soil, or a grow-bag
- the box described in the 'Square Eggs' experiment
- glue suitable for use with plastic
- string, or rubber bands
- a hand drill

What happens

If the seeds are grown properly your plants will produce nice tomatoes. By controlling the space in which they grow you can make sure the tomatoes are square instead of the usual round shape.

If possible buy some seeds from a garden shop. Follow the growing instructions to get the best results and remember to start planting the seeds in the spring. If you don't have any instructions, grow the tomatoes the same way as you grew the 'spaghetti' plants. Remember to water the plants regularly.

Wait until the plants begin to flower. If you grow them outdoors they will produce fruit all on their own. If you grow them indoors they may need a little help. You will need to tickle inside each flower with a small clean paintbrush to transfer pollen, the yellow powder in the centre of a flower, from the male part to the female part. Insects such as bees and flies do this outdoors.

Now wait until you begin to see the small, green, baby tomatoes grow inside the old flowers. This will be several weeks after the seeds have started to grow into plants. Take the small plastic box used in the 'Square Eggs' experiment and carefully drill a hole in the lid (the piece you removed from it). The hole must be big enough for the baby tomato to pass through but not more than 12mm. Glue the lid back on the box and carefully pass the baby tomato

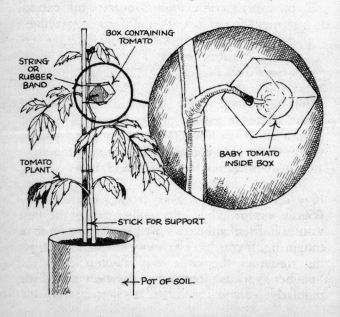

BOX CONTAINING TOMATO

STRING OR RUBBER BAND

TOMATO PLANT

BABY TOMATO INSIDE BOX

STICK FOR SUPPORT

POT OF SOIL

through the hole without knocking it off the plant. Then fix the box on the plant using string or rubber bands. Do this very carefully. Leave the box like this until the tomato fills up the box, then carefully break open the box and shake the tomato out. If it is nice and red you can eat it. Otherwise put it in a brown paper bag for a few days to let it ripen and then eat it. In either case it should be nice and square and it will fit very well into square sandwiches with square eggs. Perhaps we should call the result 'a squarewich'!

The reason you can grow a square tomato is the same as the reason you can make square eggs. Almost anything can be forced to fit into a new shape and here all we have done is let the tomato grow into a square box so it became that shape. You could do the same with other fruits or vegetables and you could also use other shapes. It's difficult to do but great fun when you succeed, so keep trying.

Sparklers ★

You will need

> a bundle of fine steel wool
> box of matches
> heat–proof mat

What happens
You can make your own flashing fireworks in a couple of minutes.

This is a sparkling experiment for November 5th and will cost you very little. It's better to do this experiment outdoors, but if it's cold and wet and you want to do it inside make sure you have plenty of space. The steel wool must be placed on a heat-proof surface well away from anything that can catch fire.

Put a thin bundle of steel wool, about 10 square centimetres, on the heat-proof mat, set a lighted match to it until the glow begins to spread, and stand well back. You will see lots of sparkles which jump around in all directions. It is sensible to have an adult present but you will do no harm if you are careful. When the sparkling has stopped, allow the black residue to cool before throwing away the ashes.

Lots of energy keeps this firework going. Iron is the main metal in steel; when you apply the flame to the steel wool the iron gains energy to combine with oxygen in the air. A chemical reaction takes place forming iron oxide. We can show this by a chemical equation called a word equation:

$$\text{iron} + \text{oxygen} \rightarrow \text{iron oxide}$$

As the iron combines with the oxygen, energy is released causing sparkles of iron oxide to leap off from the wool and helping more iron and oxygen to combine to form iron oxide. The energy is scattered about in this way until no more iron is left.

It may sound strange to you but the iron is actually burning. We think of wood, coal and candles burning, but not a metal. When wood burns it combines with oxygen to release heat energy which is exactly what happens with iron, so burning iron causes the sparkling.

That's the chemistry behind sparklers, now go ahead and enjoy them.

The Pendulum Show ★★

You will need

    a roll of thin string
    at least 28 1p coins
    coloured gum paper, or you can use felt-tip
       pens to colour white paper
    adhesive tape
    2 vertical supports, eg chair legs
    pair of scissors

What happens

A row of pendulums behaves in an unexpected way.
It will take you about twenty minutes to set it all up.

If you have ever looked at a grandfather clock you
will have noticed a large pendulum going tick-tock,
apparently forever. Hypnotists use a pendulum to
hypnotise their patients; there is something relaxing
and sleep-inducing about a slowly swinging pendulum. They have been used for water-divining, and
to try to identify the position of a disease. The
patient lies on a table and the person diagnosing the
disease holds a pendulum above various parts of the
body. If the patient is healthy the pendulum should
remain still but if an organ is diseased the pendulum
should start swinging vigorously. Nobody really
knows the why and how of this method, or even if it
does work properly, but pendulums have been used
for all sorts of purposes for many years. They can do
unexpected things, as you will see in the following
experiment.

Cut a length of string about 150 centimetres in
length. Tie the string between two vertical supports
(the legs of two chairs, or a table, for example) so it

is taut, straight and well above the ground. Then make piles of four 1p coins so you have at least five or six piles, and wrap coloured paper round each pile to make a small parcel. If you don't use sticky paper, adhesive tape will secure the paper round the coins. Each parcel of coins will act as a pendulum weight.

Cut a piece of string about 70 centimetres long and tape one end to the top of one of the weights. Tie the opposite end to the horizontal string, and you have your pendulum. Raise the weight slightly then release it so the pendulum swings in a straight line at right angles to the horizontal string. You will notice that the distance between both ends of the pendulum swing decreases until it stops altogether.

Make another pendulum which must be exactly the same length as the first one, and tie it about 10

centimetres away. Set the two pendulums at rest then raise the weight of one pendulum so it can swing as before. What happens this time? Does the pendulum stop swinging altogether? What happens to the second pendulum?

In the experiment on 'Musical Straws' you will have come across the term 'natural frequency' where objects vibrate freely at a certain frequency. The following two examples will illustrate this. There was a case of a famous opera singer who sang a certain note which smashed a wine-glass in the room. The note caused the air to vibrate at a frequency which coincided with the natural frequency of the particles of glass. This caused the glass to vibrate so violently that it broke. This phenomenon is known as resonance, where the frequency of the force applied to an object, like the glass, is equal to its natural frequency. Another example of resonance occurs when a regiment of soldiers march across a wooden bridge. In this case there is a danger that the frequency of the soldiers' steps will equal the natural frequency of the wood, causing it to smash, so soldiers march at different speeds when they cross a bridge.

When the first pendulum is swinging, the horizontal string starts vibrating. These vibrations pass along to the second pendulum until resonance occurs, and it starts to swing. The first pendulum loses its energy as the other is set into motion. Now, make more pendulums by taping equal lengths of string to each parcel of coins and tying the pendulums 10 centimetres apart from one another. Set one pendulum swinging and the show will start. Resonance occurs only when the pendulums are all the same length. See what happens when they are different lengths.

Potty Paper   ★★

You will need

> some paper
> a pencil or pen
> adhesive tape or glue
> scissors

What happens

You build a paper shape. When you cut it you get a surprise. You can do this experiment in only a few minutes.

Cut your paper into one or more strips, each about 3 centimetres wide and 15 centimetres long. Make a small V-shaped cut at each end of the paper and draw a line, from one cut to the other, on *both* sides of the paper. On *one* side only, draw a cross at each end of the paper (fig 1).

Have the adhesive tape or glue ready. Take the strip of paper and twist it once, then bend it round to make a band with the two crosses facing each other (fig 2). Now stick the band together using the adhesive tape or glue. If you do this correctly you will not be able to see the crosses when you have finished.

When the band is stuck together take the scissors and cut along the line you drew (fig 3), but before you finish try and guess what will happen.

This type of band is called a Möbius strip. It is strange because it is twisted. Just that simple twist means that what looks like becoming two rings of paper in fact becomes one. Some scientists study shapes like these. They are called topologists and their science is topology, the study of surfaces.

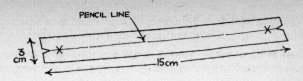

PENCIL LINE

3 cm

15 cm

1. A VIEW OF THE TOP SIDE OF YOUR STRIP OF PAPER

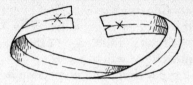

2. MAKE A BEND BY GIVING THE PAPER JUST ONE TWIST AND JOINING THE CROSSES TOGETHER

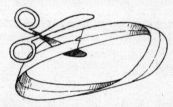

3. GLUE THE BAND TOGETHER AND CUT ALONG THE PENCIL LINE

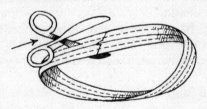

4. TRY CUTTING A NEW BAND IN THIS WAY. KEEP THE SCISSORS BETWEEN THE EDGE OF THE PAPER AND THE PENCIL LINE YOU DREW. THE DOTTED LINE SHOWS YOU ROUGHLY WHERE TO CUT.

They spend lots of time trying to imagine what things will look like when they turn them inside out!

If you found this experiment intriguing, try these other simple experiments. First, try cutting a band with one twist in half, as described above. Then cut the result in half again but try to guess what will happen first. Another experiment is to cut a twisted band into thirds. Keep the scissors half way between the line you drew and the edge of the paper (fig 4). Can you guess what will happen?

See 'Tying Yourself in Knots' on page 12 for a very different experiment involving topology.

It Rolls Uphill ★★

You will need

> 2 identical plastic kitchen funnels each approximately 11½ cm in diameter
> some rubber or silicon-type glue (eg cow gum)
> cotton thread
> 2 stiff pieces of wood, each at least 90cm long
> 1 block of wood, 10cm high (or books)
> 2 blocks of wood, each 14cm high (or books)
> a ruler
> a table knife

What happens

You will see that some things really can roll up a hill. It only takes a few minutes to do but you must allow time for the glue to dry, probably at least an hour.

Your two funnels can be either of the types shown in figure 1, but they must both be the same so that they balance. Start by gluing two bits of cotton across the top of one funnel to form a cross (fig 2). Then glue the two funnels together (fig 3). Leave the glue to dry. Put the three blocks of wood (or books) on the floor or on a table. The short one (10 centimetres high) should be near to you. The other two should both be 85 centimetres away from the short one and 40 centimetres apart. Put the two long pieces of wood on top of the blocks to make two runners or rails (fig 4). You may need to use a drop of glue to hold each one still.

As you can see, you've built a hill. If you try to roll a cardboard tube on the hill it will always roll down the hill (unless you cheat). Try putting the glued funnels at the bottom of the hill and see what happens.

The result is unbelievable, but it's not a trick. It really does happen, because of one of the laws in the science of physics. This law says that the centre of gravity of any object will always try to move downwards. What is the centre of gravity? The answer to this question is best explained by another simple experiment. Pick up a ruler with your thumb and one other finger, holding it lightly towards one end. The other end will drop down. Now hold it lightly in the middle. Eventually you will find where to hold it so that it balances on your thumb and stays still. That point is the centre of gravity of the ruler. Now try doing the same with the table knife and you will probably find that the centre of gravity isn't the middle.

Now return to the funnels. Put them on the bottom of the hill again and wait until they stop rolling. Then look through the spout of one and you will see the cotton cross. Carefully measure how high the cross is from the floor or table. Write down

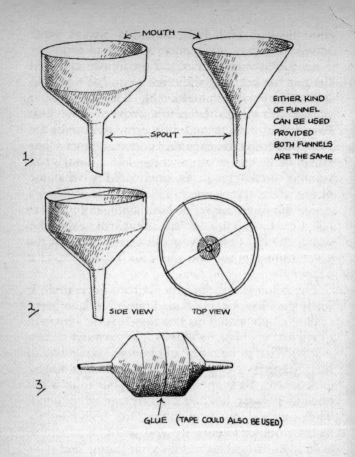

MOUTH

EITHER KIND
OF FUNNEL
CAN BE USED
PROVIDED
BOTH FUNNELS
ARE THE SAME

SPOUT

1,

SIDE VIEW   TOP VIEW

2,

3,

GLUE (TAPE COULD ALSO BE USED)

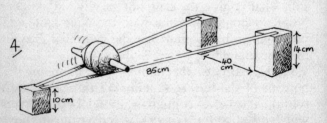

4,

10cm   85cm   40 cm   14cm

your answer. (All good scientists always write down what they see because it's easy to forget or remember wrongly.) Take off the funnels and hold them at the bottom of the hill. You have to hold them as they are unstable like this. Keep holding and measure how high the cotton cross is now. You should find that although it is at the bottom of the hill, the cotton cross is higher now than when it has rolled up the hill. In other words, as the funnels roll up, the cotton cross rolls down. Guess what the cotton cross represents? That's right. It shows where the centre of gravity of the joined funnels is and, as you can see, it has obeyed the rules and moved down. This only works because the funnels have sloping sides, and the sides have to have a steeper slope than the hill.

Try this on your friends. Even when you see it happen it's hard to believe, isn't it?

Where Am I? ★

You will need

> 2 sticks each about 30cm long
> string
> chalk if available
> 2 small stones
> a flat area of ground

What happens
You will learn how to find out which way is north without a watch, a compass or even looking at trees to see which side the moss is growing. It can take a few hours but most of that is just watching.

On a sunny morning go outside and push one of the sticks into the ground so it is upright. This stick will act as a shadow-maker. Look at the shadow the stick makes and put a stone or something at the end of the shadow, then watch for a bit to make sure the shadow is getting shorter. It will do this all morning. Tie some string to the bottom of the stick and then tie another stick or piece of chalk to the free end of the string. The chalk or loose stick must just touch the stone marking the end of the longest shadow when the string is tight. Use the chalk or stick to draw an arc (fig 1). It must still be morning.

Wait for a time and watch the shadow get shorter until it stops touching the arc. After that it will start to get longer until eventually it touches the arc again. Use another stone to mark where the shadow touches the arc again.

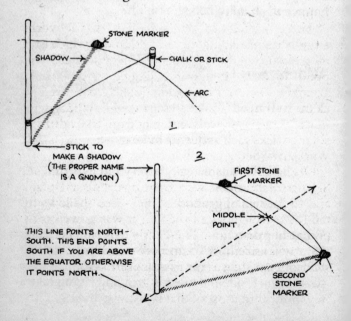

Using some more string find the midway point on the ground between the two stones. A line made from this middle point to the shadow-maker stick (fig 2) will point north–south. In the northern hemisphere the end touching the arc will point north. In the southern hemisphere it will point south.

This method of finding north works because of the movement of the sun. It rises in the east and gets higher during the day until it reaches its highest point and then starts going down to set in the west. So the 'west', 'high' and 'east' points can be thought of as three points of a triangle. With the stick you can use the sun to cut this triangle in half. If you stand still in one place and point exactly between east and west you will then be pointing either north or south. The sun and the stick make a shadow pointer to do this for you.

The advantage of this system is that it works anywhere, providing the sun is shining, which isn't always true of a compass. A compass needle will point towards anything magnetic so it is only accurate when not near to large pieces of metal or electric motors. Compasses also point to 'magnetic north' which is slightly different from true north. A solar compass isn't affected by magnetism so it will work anywhere.

Once again, this is really a very old experiment. Similar experiments were done by druids in Britain and the ancient Egyptians. They used shadows to tell them which day of the year it was as well as to point out a direction. These early experiments gave rise to the science of astronomy and even today, shadows can still supply useful information.

The Crystal Set ★★★★

You will need

- 1 ferrite rod aerial (medium wave only)
- 1 crystal earplug
- 1 socket for crystal earplug
- 1 variable capacitor 500 pF
- 1 capacitor 100 pF
- 1 diode OA91 or equivalent
- 10 metres or more of single core electrical wire (eg bell wire)
- electrical wire for connecting the parts above
- soldering iron and solder (but keep reading if you can't get these)
- some cardboard from an old box (eg shoe box)
- a pin or needle
- pliers or paperclips if available

What happens

In about an hour you will be able to build your own radio – and it doesn't need batteries!

If you do not have a soldering iron don't worry, the radio can be built without one, but it is a lot better and more reliable if you do use solder. Figure 1 shows you what each part looks like and figure 2 shows a 'wiring diagram'. Begin with the variable capacitor. Fix it to the cardboard base by using the screws that came with it or by pushing the two prongs A and B through holes made with a pin. The variable capacitor may have three prongs but, if it does, two will be the same, so in this case only use one of the two identical ones. Now take the diode, bend the ends over carefully and push these through the card. The diode is shaped like a bullet. Make sure the wire (C) from the flat end is near to the variable capacitor. Solder C to A. Be very careful when using a soldering iron, if possible get an adult to help you. Hold wire C with pliers or put a paper clip on the wire while you solder it. If you don't have a soldering iron just clip the wires together. Either use a paper clip or a grip binder (fig 3).

Now join all the other parts together in the same way so that underneath the card looks like figure 4. Try to follow the wiring diagram in figure 2 at the same time. You should end up with all the wires and joins underneath the cardboard but all the electronic components on top. When soldering, always try to hold both wires with a paper clip or pliers. This stops heat from travelling along the wire and burning the resistor or diode. It's called a heat sink.

Finally, you will need some bell wire. Solder or join a short length, about 1 metre, to one connector on the ferrite rod aerial. This is the 'earth'. Solder or join as much wire as possible to the other connector to act as the aerial. It must be at least 10 metres long, but 20 metres is better.

To operate your radio, plug in the earphone. Bare the wire at the unattached end of the earth and attach it to a cold water pipe or central heating pipe. The long aerial wire should be as high up as possible. The best idea is to attach the far end to a tree. Now very slowly turn the knob on the variable capacitor. If you've done everything correctly, you will pick up the strongest radio station in your area. If you're really lucky you may get two or even three stations.

This is a modern version of the original crystal radio. In the science of electronics the 'crystal' is now called a diode. If your dad or grandad built a set he may remember using a cat's whisker to tune it!

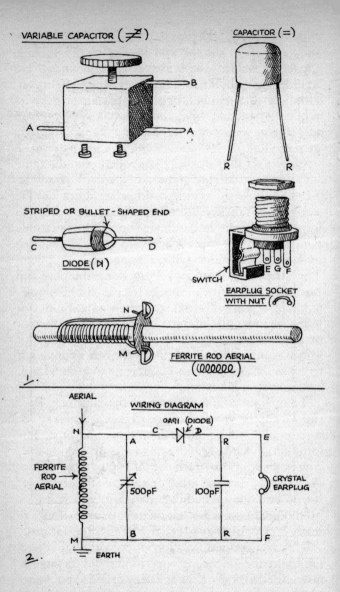

VARIABLE CAPACITOR ($\neq$)

CAPACITOR (=)

A   A

B

R   R

STRIPED OR BULLET - SHAPED END

C   D

DIODE (▷|)

SWITCH

E G F

EARPLUG SOCKET
WITH NUT (⌒)

N

M

FERRITE ROD AERIAL
(◠◠◠◠◠◠)

1.

AERIAL

WIRING DIAGRAM

OA91 (DIODE)

N

C ▷|◁ D

A   R   E

FERRITE
ROD
AERIAL

500pF   100pF

CRYSTAL
EARPLUG

B   R   F

M

EARTH

2.

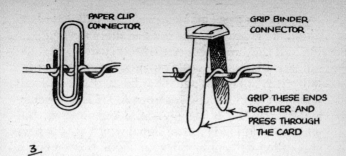

PAPER CLIP
CONNECTOR

GRIP BINDER
CONNECTOR

GRIP THESE ENDS
TOGETHER AND
PRESS THROUGH
THE CARD

3

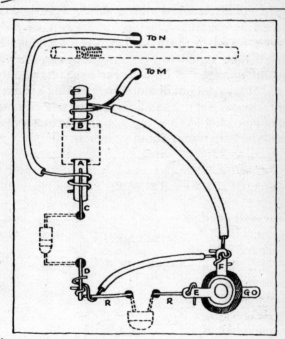

To N

To M

B

A

C

D

F

E

GO

R   R

4 A DIAGRAM SHOWING HOW ALL THE WIRES CONNECT
TOGETHER <u>UNDERNEATH</u> THE CARDBOARD.
MAKE ALL THE CONNECTIONS BY USING SOLDER OR
THE CLIPS SHOWN IN FIG 3.

Now we use the variable capacitor. Radio waves in the air are received in the form of alternating current (AC). If they are changed to direct current (DC) we can get a copy of whatever programme the radio station is broadcasting. The diode is the 'crystal' which changes the current from AC to DC. Changing AC to DC is usually called rectification, but when it is done to create a signal which we can hear it is called detection. So your diode is detecting a signal collected by the long aerial. The signal is carried as electricity, a type of energy, or radio waves, which are just another type of energy. To get a louder signal you need more energy. So you can either collect more with perhaps 200 metres of aerial or you can put in more energy using a battery. Our 'crystal' set doesn't need a battery because the aerial is so long. And as you don't need a battery you won't have to worry about switching off.

The Chemical Cabbage ★★

You will need

> a red cabbage
> bicarbonate of soda
> a lemon
> 3 empty jam-jars
> a saucepan
> an old teaspoon, or spatula
> an old cup or glass
> a cooker ring

What happens
Have you heard that acids are nasty liquids which burn you? Well, that's only partly true. Some acids

are dangerous and should be treated with the greatest respect, but others are quite harmless and you will even find them in your food. This experiment is a safe, colourful test to help you discover the acids in your home. It will take you five minutes to prove the point but you can go on experimenting as long as you like.

Question: what is the connection between a small, fungus-like plant that grows in Holland and a very famous paper used by chemists?

Answer: litmus. No chemistry laboratory is complete without litmus paper and litmus is extracted from these Dutch plants. Litmus is very useful to chemists because it always turns red when you add it to an acid, and it turns blue with a base, but more about bases later.

Acids are very important chemicals. They are found not only in the laboratory but also around the house and in your food. You won't have to go to a chemist or Holland to find out what acids you have at home – a red cabbage will tell you.

Squeeze the juice from a lemon into a clean jam-jar. Add water until the jar is half-full, and stir. Pour water into the next jam-jar until it is half-full. In the third jar put half a teaspoon of bicarbonate of soda, add water to the half-way mark and stir until you have dissolved the powder. Now set the jam-jars side by side.

Place small pieces of red cabbage in a saucepan and add a little water. Heat gently for five or ten minutes, allow to cool and pour the violet cabbage water into a cup or glass. Pour a little of this cabbage water into each of the three jam-jars and, abracadabra! The lemon water goes red, the plain water turns violet, and the bicarbonate of soda solution turns green.

Substances like litmus and red cabbage water are called indicators. They indicate to us whether substances are acids or bases. Water from red cabbage always turns red when added to an acid and green if added to a base. But, what is a base? To find out, add some red cabbage indicator to some more lemon water then add about a teaspoonful of bicarbonate of soda. Carry on adding the bicarbonate of soda until you see a change. The indicator colour will change from red, through violet to green. A base, in this case bicarbonate of soda, is a substance that can change an acid to form water plus a substance called a salt, and chemists say that a base neutralises an acid. Substances that are neither acids nor bases are neutral, so water is an example of a neutral substance.

On a clean sheet of paper draw five columns as below and write in the headings. Write up the three substances you have tested as examples.

substance	colour of indicator	acid	neutral	base
lemon juice	red	√	X	X
water	violet	X	√	X
bicarbonate of soda solution	green	X	X	√

Continue by testing other substances and recording your results. Use the red cabbage indicator to sort out all the acids, bases and neutral substances in your house. Make sure you wash your containers thoroughly after each experiment, otherwise an acid, say, may remain in the container and ruin the result of the next test. Two common substances worth testing are white vinegar and washing-soda crystals. Remember three points before you start:

1 Don't handle the substances you test unless you know they are safe. Pour them gently into the container.
2 If you test tablets, powders, crystals or any other solids, dissolve them in water first.
3 Use only colourless liquids for your tests otherwise you won't be able to detect the colour change.

If you can get a beetroot, use beetroot juice as an indicator. Some other vegetables and also flower petals can be used as indicators. Try and discover which ones they are.

You may like to know the names of some of the important acids and bases you will find in a laboratory. The main acids are: hydrochloric acid, sulphuric acid and nitric acid (these are strong acids which could burn you badly if you touched them). The main bases are: sodium hydroxide, ammonium hydroxide and lime-water. Many acids and bases are used in industry to manufacture such important products as fertilisers and detergents.

The Cheeky Water Pistol   ★★

You will need

>   a clean bottle, such as a small milk bottle
>   a cork or rubber bung with a hole in it
>   a plastic ballpoint pen casing or plastic straw to
>   fit the hole
>   a cardboard box, about the size of the bottle

What happens

You'll surprise a friend, but make sure he can take a joke because he may get rather wet. This only takes a few minutes.

Take the clean bottle and fill it almost to the top with tap-water. Push the pen or straw through the cork. You can get a cork with a hole from shops that sell wine-making kits, or a science teacher at school might help you. Make sure the ballpoint pen casing fits tightly in the cork. Then push the cork into the bottle. Make a small hole in one end of the cardboard box and put the bottle in the box so that the pen fits through the hole in it. Close the box and all you should see is a box with a pen fitted to it.

Ask a friend to blow very hard down the pen. When he stops blowing, water will immediately

HARD PLASTIC STRAW

RUBBER BUNG

WATER

HIDE THE BOTTLE IN A BOX

rush up the tube. If he has taken his lips off the pen he'll get a face full of water. Otherwise, he'll get a mouthful.

If you try this without the box you will understand it better. When you blow down the pen you will see bubbles going into the water. Some of these bubbles of air dissolve in the water. This is just like the gas dissolved in fizzy drinks which you saw in the 'Lemonade Factory' experiment on page 20. The rest of the air that you have blown down the pen rises up to join the air between the cork and the water. Now there is more air in the bottle than there was before but it doesn't take up any extra space yet. It keeps trying to by pressing down on the water. As soon as you stop blowing more air in, the air already in the bottle will press the water back up the pen so that it makes a water fountain.

Probably the most important thing to learn from this experiment is that the extra air you blow in can fit into the same space as the air already in the bottle. This is because you can squeeze a given amount of gas, which takes up a certain space, into a smaller space. This is usually called compression. For example, if you put your finger on the end of a bicycle pump you can compress the air inside it by pushing the pump. If you fill the pump with water you will find it impossible to compress. Gases compress, liquids do not.

Germs *

You will need

some wine (white or red)
a clean bottle or jar

What happens

The wine will turn to vinegar in about three days.
This experiment takes only a few seconds to
prepare.

Take some wine, preferably some that you made
in the experiment, 'It's Alive', (page 53) and put it in
a clean bottle. Do not put a top on the bottle, just
leave it open in a warm room, somewhere where it
will not be in anyone's way. Once a day go back to
the wine and have a careful smell. After a few days
you will notice the wine no longer smells pleasant
and fruity. Instead it will have a sharp or acid smell
as it will have turned to vinegar.

This change is brought about by tiny living
organisms, so small that we need a microscope to
see them. The organisms are called bacteria and the
name given to the bacteria responsible for changing
wine to vinegar is *Mycoderma acetii*. The presence of
these bacteria causes oxygen from the air to react
with the alcohol in the wine. This chemical reaction
produces acetic acid which dissolves in the rest of
the wine to make wine vinegar. You can use this
vinegar in cooking if you like.

As you can see, these bacteria have been very
helpful in producing something we use for food.
Other bacteria are also useful, for example in
making cheese or yogurt, but not all bacteria help
us. Many of them cause diseases in plants or

animals, including ourselves. Doctors call these bacteria by their Latin names but we often use an easier word – 'germs'. It isn't a very good word as it can be very misleading. After all, we've just seen how useful some germs can be.

Living Food ★★

You will need

  a tablespoon
  a small carton of natural yogurt
  a pint of milk
  a gas ring
  a saucepan
  large covered bowl
  refrigerator

What happens
If you like yogurt then this is just the project for you; if you don't, read on anyway because you will be learning about the fascinating science of bacteriology. The yogurt will take a day or two to settle to the right consistency, but it takes only about twenty minutes to prepare.

The Turks are credited with the discovery of yogurt but its use in the kitchen was widespread in ancient times as it is a refreshing food full of good nourishment. The secret behind making yogurt is that it is a living culture as well as a food. A spoonful of yogurt contains thousands of tiny living organisms called bacteria. We came across bacteria in the previous experiment and learned that there are many different kinds. Many are useful to human beings, in the manufacture and processing of food as well as agriculture and sanitation, but unfortunately, many kinds are dangerous and are the cause of disease. Two kinds of harmless bacteria are responsible for the taste and flavour of yogurt and they are called *Lactobacillus bulgaricus* and *Streptococcus thermophilus*.

We can produce more yogurt from yogurt because bacteria can increase their numbers very quickly. They do this by splitting in two. Bacteria can split in two once every twenty minutes, so in one day one bacterium could produce 4,700,000,000,000,000,000,000 new bacteria! Can you imagine how many bacteria there would be if you started off with millions? However, bacteria can only survive and divide if they are kept at the right temperature. Bacteriologists are scientists who study bacteria and find out what conditions they flourish in. When the temperature is too high or too low, the bacteria may become dormant or die.

Lactobacillus bulgaricus grows best between 45°C and 47°C, whereas *Streptococcus thermophilus* enjoys the temperature range between 38°C and 42°C, so we have to control the temperature of the yogurt very carefully. We could use a thermometer and special yogurt-making equipment but it's more fun to experiment and improvise.

Put two tablespoonfuls of yogurt in a large bowl. Pour a pint of milk into a saucepan and heat until boiling. Allow the milk to cool until it is slightly above 'blood' temperature. This means it should just be cool enough to place your finger in the milk for ten seconds. Don't burn your finger testing it! Pour the milk over the yogurt and stir. Cover the bowl and leave in a warm place for the next five hours so the yogurt is warm enough to keep the two kinds of bacteria living and dividing; the temperature should stay very near to that of the warm milk. You will have to decide for yourself the best way to do this in your home. If it's a warm day you could leave the bowl near a window which captures the sun, or you could wrap the bowl with soft material to retain the heat, or leave it on a low setting in the oven.

After five hours or so in the warmth, the new yogurt should be on its way, but you will need to leave it for a day so it can reach the right thickness or consistency. After a day it should be just right, if not, leave it a little longer or try again.

Once your yogurt is ready you can eat it as it is or stir in a little honey and it should taste delicious. If you want to keep it, store it in the refrigerator. Another beautiful yogurt concoction is an Indian drink called 'lassi'.To make this, add a cupful of milk or water to three spoons of yogurt with honey, and mix in a blender. And, remember, you can make even more yogurt from that which you have just prepared, all you have to do is help the bacteria split in two.

Bacteria are not the only living things that are important in producing food and drinks. Yeast is another very valuable little organism as you can see in the experiment 'It's Alive' on page 53. Believe it or not, every week of your life you consume millions of tiny living organisms as well as the food and drink they help to produce. Enjoy eating your bacteria!

A Home-made Camera ★★★★

You will need

C126 film and the box it comes in
some cardboard (such as a cereal box or shoe-
box)
glue for paper
silicon rubber glue
scissors or a knife
ruler and pencil
black sticky tape (insulating tape)
small spice box (or any small cardboard or
plastic box with a removable lid)
black paint and a brush
a flattened milk-bottle top or a piece of thick
cooking foil
a needle

What happens

You can make a simple pinhole camera that costs
almost nothing but can still take good photographs.
This is very difficult so expect to take several hours
to make a really good job of it.

Begin by making a box. Draw the pattern shown in
figure 1 on your cardboard. Each side of the squares
measures 8 centimetres; the size of the flaps is not
too important but they should be at least 1 centimetre wide. Cut out the pattern in one piece, and
remember to cut out the two holes as well. Then use
the back of the scissors or the knife to score along
the dotted lines so that the cardboard is easy to fold.
Now fold the pattern to make a box. When you are
sure it fits together, stick it together leaving one side
open. Leave the glue to dry and then paint the inside

black including the side that is still open.

Next take your milk-bottle top or piece of foil and make a hole in it with a needle. The pinhole must be as small as possible. Use the black sticky tape to stick the foil inside the box so the pinhole is right in the middle of the 1-centimetre square hole (fig 2).

Cut out the bottom of the small box, then glue this box to the outside of the other box, over the 1-centimetre square hole (fig 3). You will use this as a 'shutter' by taking the lid off for different amounts of time. When you are sure everything is stuck well you can close the last side of your big box, glue it, and tape up all the edges on the outside with black tape.

Take the box containing the film cartridge and open it carefully at one end. Remove the packet of film but keep the box. Cut two holes in the box as shown in figures 4 and 5. Carefully open the other end of the box. Then cut open the front of the box along the lines shown in figure 6. Open the packet of film and put the film inside the cut box. You will be able to see the little arrow in the window of the film cartridge through the window in your box. Use silicon rubber glue to stick the flat side of the cartridge tightly to the box. You can see the film if you look at the cartridge carefully – it looks grey and shiny. Now stick the box of film to the back of the camera. The two flaps must be open and must go over the space in the back of the camera (fig 7). Then stick tape over the box of film so that no light can get in anywhere, but do leave the back window uncovered so that you will be able to see how many pictures you have taken. Leave the penny-size hole uncovered too.

The camera is now ready. To take a photograph

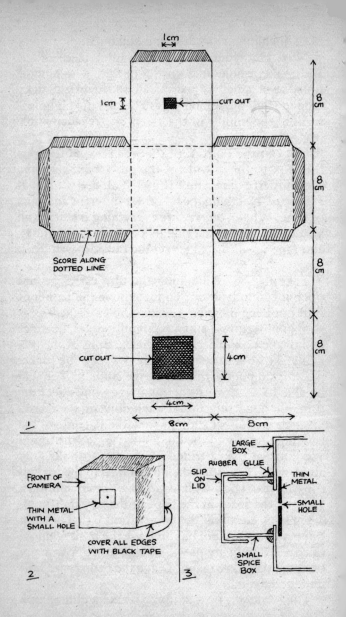

1cm

1cm ↕ ◄— CUT OUT

8 cm

8 cm

SCORE ALONG
DOTTED LINE

8 cm

8 cm

CUT OUT —►   4cm

4cm

8cm   8cm

1

FRONT OF
CAMERA

THIN METAL
WITH A
SMALL HOLE

COVER ALL EDGES
WITH BLACK TAPE

2

LARGE
BOX

RUBBER GLUE

SLIP
ON
LID

THIN
METAL

SMALL
HOLE

SMALL
SPICE BOX

3

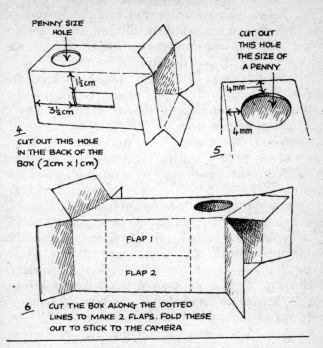

PENNY SIZE HOLE

1½cm

3½cm

4 CUT OUT THIS HOLE IN THE BACK OF THE BOX (2cm × 1cm)

CUT OUT THIS HOLE THE SIZE OF A PENNY

4mm

4mm

5

FLAP 1

FLAP 2

6 CUT THE BOX ALONG THE DOTTED LINES TO MAKE 2 FLAPS. FOLD THESE OUT TO STICK TO THE CAMERA

7 THIS SHOWS THE BACK OF THE CAMERA

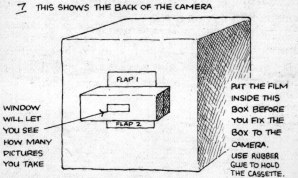

FLAP 1

FLAP 2

WINDOW WILL LET YOU SEE HOW MANY PICTURES YOU TAKE

PUT THE FILM INSIDE THIS BOX BEFORE YOU FIX THE BOX TO THE CAMERA. USE RUBBER GLUE TO HOLD THE CASSETTE.

you must put the camera on a firm surface such as a chair or the floor and point it at an object at least 10 metres away. By putting your finger in the penny-size hole you can wind the film on until the next number is in the correct position. Then with the camera absolutely still you must remove the cover on the spice box. The length of time you leave the film exposed to the light varies according to the brightness or otherwise of the day and you will have to experiment at first. Try working outdoors on a sunny day and leaving the film exposed for three, six, nine, twelve or fifteen seconds. When enough time has passed put the lid back on and wind on the film ready to take the next photograph. Take several photographs using different exposure times. Write down what you have done so you can check the results and learn by your experiences. Take the film to a camera shop (not a chemist) and tell the people there what you have done. Ask them to develop the film for you. A good shop will have people who are very helpful and who will be willing to spend time with you or even want to see your camera. Have a chat with them and let them advise you. With lots of practice and patience you should get some very good results.

Although some of the experiments on the next few pages can be done at home, you will probably get better results if you do them at school.

Making Paint   ★★★   S

You will need

Fehling's solution
glucose
ammonium dichromate crystals
liquid gum
bunsen burner
filter funnel and filter paper (or kitchen towel)
an egg, if possible
a test-tube
a stand, clamp, boss, tripod and gauze
a small beaker
a round-bottomed flask

What happens

Using the chemicals above you can make two colours to use for painting. It takes less than thirty minutes but you will need to do it at school as you will need to ask the teacher for the chemicals. Your paint will be best if it is left to dry a little before using.

Put about half a teaspoon of glucose in the beaker and add half a test-tube of the blue Fehling's solution. Then add about half a test-tube of water. Gently shake the beaker until the glucose dissolves. Place the beaker on a tripod and gauze and then carefully warm the mixture over a very low flame. Do not let it boil or you will make a useless sticky mess. If it does begin to bubble, take the beaker off the heat until the bubbling stops, then try again. If you heat the mixture correctly, the liquid will turn green, yellow, orange and then red.

When you see the red colour, stop heating and let

the mixture cool down. Now pour it into a filter paper (or if you don't have one pour it slowly on to a wad of absorbent paper) in a filter funnel over a container or sink. Let all the water run off, then gently pour on some fresh water to wash the red paste. Do this two or three times. Your red paint is now ready to mix. At first, it will be wet and sticky and you can either use it like this or let it dry to a powder. When it has dried, you can use it by adding one or two drops of liquid gum to it. You can also add a drop or two of water if you need to. You will now have made a good red paint which you can use as normal. It is a result of a chemical reaction between glucose and Fehling's solution.

If you look at very old manuscripts, the colour of illuminated letters is usually still bright. This is because the scribes who painted the letters added egg yolk to their paint. If you want to, try adding a

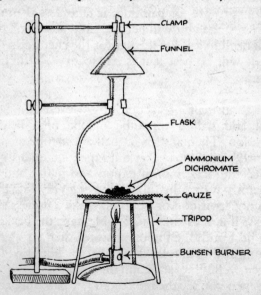

CLAMP

FUNNEL

FLASK

AMMONIUM DICHROMATE

GAUZE

TRIPOD

BUNSEN BURNER

drop of egg yolk to your paint before you use it. Make sure you use only the yolk though, and do not mix it with the egg white.

To make a second colour, put a few ammonium dichromate crystals in a round-bottomed flask. Cover the top of the flask by clamping a funnel upside down above it (see diagram) and heat the flask very gently. Then stand back and watch what happens. This reaction gives off a gas called nitrogen leaving a green powder, chromium oxide, behind. You can use the powder as paint by adding gum, with or without water, and some egg yolk.

In ancient times only a few of these true pigments could be made. A true pigment is a chemical that will not dissolve in water and glue. Today we know a lot more about chemistry and can make many different true pigments.

Try asking your teacher for advice about making other colours. You could also try using chalk and gum for white paint and powdered coal, or char-coal, and gum for black paint.

Invisible Ink   ★★   S

You will need

At home
   a lemon
   an instrument which you can use as a pen, such as an old fountain pen or a glass rod. Don't use a new pen.
   an old cup or beaker
   a source of heat, eg a radiator, bunsen burner, or a small flame on a gas ring
   a piece of white paper

At school
> cobalt chloride crystals
> a small beaker
> a glass stirring rod

What happens

You can send secret messages to your friends, who will watch with wonder as a plain sheet of paper becomes full of writing. It will take you only a few minutes to prepare your invisible ink.

Inks date back to 2500 BC when they were used by the ancient Egyptians and Chinese to inscribe parchment scrolls. Ink was a useful invention because it was permanent, simple to use and a great improvement on hammering messages into stone. We do not know for certain when an ink was invented which could appear and disappear. Spies in ancient times would have found it extremely useful, and an excellent source of invisible ink was available at least 1000 years ago. This source was our old acidic friend – the lemon.

Dip your 'pen' into some juice from a lemon and write a message on a piece of paper. Let the juice dry then hold the paper up to the light. You will notice it is transparent where the lemon juice has touched it. Get an adult to warm the paper above a small flame and in a few minutes your writing appears in brown. Take care not to burn the paper when warming it.

When you apply heat to the paper, the transparent, lemon juice part singes more quickly than the rest of the paper and shows up as a brown colour. In this way, lemon juice can appear as writing when heated, but you can't make it disappear. A substance that can do a combined appearing-disappearing act is the chemical cobalt chloride; you will have to try this in school.

If your school has a chemistry laboratory ask your teacher for about half a dozen small crystals of cobalt chloride in a small beaker. Dissolve the crystals in half a beaker of water and you will get a pink solution. This is your invisible ink. Write a message on a piece of paper and you will find it very difficult to distinguish your writing from the blank part of the paper. Warm the message well above a small flame until it is completely dry. What colour do you see now? Go over your visible writing with a little water and it should vanish.

Cobalt chloride is a chemical that can form a 'complex' with water. In other words, the water and cobalt chloride link up. The colour of this complex is pink. On heating, the water is driven off leaving behind the dry cobalt chloride which is blue.

Clean Money ★★★ S

You will need

> 2 tarnished copper coins, eg 2p pieces
> 2 lengths of insulated wire (each about 60cm) with crocodile clips attached
> retort stand with boss and clamp
> small beaker
> copper sulphate crystals
> battery (4 to 6 volts)
> old spoon or spatula
> glass rod
> detergent
> old cloth

What happens
Your copper coins will look brand new. It will take you about twenty minutes to put a shine on them.

Take the two tarnished copper coins and wash them in soapy water to remove any grease which may prevent a good electrical contact. Dry the coins with an old cloth, and connect one end of each length of wire to the edge of each coin by means of crocodile clips. Place a spoonful or spatula-full of copper sulphate crystals in the beaker, add water until it is half-full and stir with the glass rod to dissolve all the crystals. Connect the free ends of each wire to the battery. Immerse the coins in the copper sulphate solution, making sure they do not touch, and support the connecting wires by a clamp on the retort

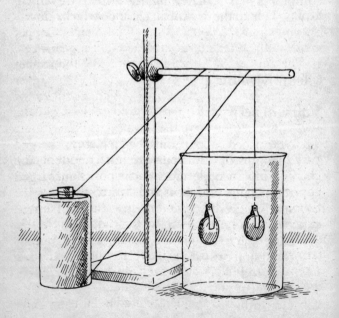

stand. Leave the coins in the solution for about twenty minutes. After you have 'plated' the coins wipe them again with the old cloth and they should look almost new.

Why does copper tarnish in the first place? Well, copper does not react with many chemicals but it can combine very slowly with oxygen in the air. You may have heard the word 'react' before, but it has a special meaning for the scientist. Briefly, when substances react a change of energy takes place and new substances are formed. In this case, copper reacts with oxygen to form a new substance called copper oxide. We can show this by an equation:

$$\text{copper} + \text{oxygen} \rightarrow \text{copper oxide}$$

You will see a similar equation in the experiment, 'Sparklers' (on page 59). Only the surface copper reacts with the oxygen and it happens very slowly so you can't see the reaction taking place. Copper oxide is black and gives the coin its dull appearance.

The aim of the experiment is to coat the copper oxide with a layer of fresh copper metal. The copper sulphate solution contains charged particles of copper called ions. Copper ions do not look like the metal, in fact they give the solution its blue colour. The electric current is a flow of tiny charged particles, called electrons, which removes the charge from the copper ions and deposits uncharged copper metal on the coin attached to the negative terminal of the battery. (See the 'Bionic Lemon' experiment, page 98, for how to produce an electric current). When this coin is plated, attach another tarnished coin to the negative terminal and start again. Meanwhile, note what happens to the coin on the positive terminal.

Metal–plating is frequently used in industry. The

most common form of plating occurs in the production of tin cans. There is not much tin in tin cans because it is an expensive metal; the main metal used is iron. The tin is plated on to the iron to prevent rusting, so really they should be called iron cans. Chromium, nickel, aluminium, silver and gold are all metals used for plating, but don't try gold plating – it's a very skilled job and you won't be very happy if it doesn't work!

The Bionic Lemon   ***   s

You will need

At home
- a lemon
- a copper coin, eg a 2p piece
- a piece of aluminium cooking foil, about 2 sq cm
- a small knife
- a length of fuse wire
- a small speaker – you could use a speaker from an old or broken transistor radio

At school
- a milliammeter
- a large beaker
- a 1.5V light bulb in a bulb holder
- connecting wires, with crocodile clips attached
- a large cleaned copper plate
- a large zinc plate
- dilute hydrochloric acid
- potassium dichromate solution

What happens

Have you ever thought of using a lemon as a source of electricity? Well, here's a way to construct a rather unusual battery which can generate a tiny electric current; it will take you only a few minutes to find out how.

One evening, about two hundred years ago, the Italian biologist, Professor Galvani, left a dissected frog in salt solution to preserve it overnight. Galvani was rather absent-minded, and as he rose from his stool a couple of coins fell out of his pocket into the dish containing the frog. Galvani forgot to pick them up – an historic lapse of memory. After breakfast the next morning Galvani returned to the frog, and to his horror and amazement, saw the dead and dissected animal jumping about in the dish. He took a closer look at the frog. When he removed one of the coins the creature stopped jumping and twitching. Galvani was about to make a great scientific discovery. He performed further experiments and found, together with his friend and rival, Volta, that, if two different metals are placed in a solution which allows electricity to pass through it, then an electric current can be produced. It was a flow of electricity that excited the nerves of the frog and caused the leg muscles to twitch. Salt solution can conduct electricity and any solution which does this is called an electrolyte.

They did not know it at the time, but Galvani and Volta had discovered the battery. You can make your own very weak battery with a lemon because the juice within a lemon is an electrolyte. First, make two large slits, about one centimetre apart, in a nice juicy lemon (fig 1). In one slit place a clean, shiny copper coin and, in the other, the flat piece of

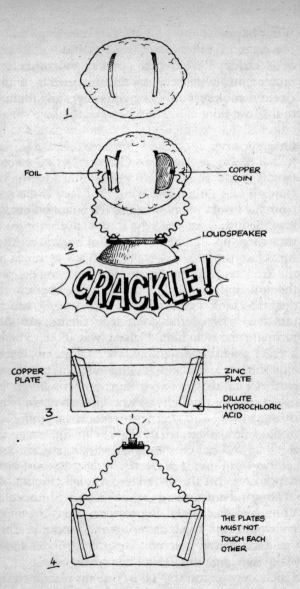

1

FOIL

COPPER COIN

LOUDSPEAKER

2

CRACKLE!

COPPER PLATE

ZINC PLATE

DILUTE HYDROCHLORIC ACID

3

THE PLATES MUST NOT TOUCH EACH OTHER

4

cooking foil. Connect the coin and cooking foil by fuse wire to your speaker (fig 2). You will hear a loud crackle. Remove the speaker and connect a piece of fuse-wire between the two metals, ie the coin and cooking foil. Place the tip of your tongue on the fuse-wire and you will feel a tingling which indicates that a small electric current is flowing through the wire.

You might like to know the size of the electric current produced by your lemon. Take it to school and insert the two metals. Ask your science teacher to connect them to a milliammeter. You will see a large deflection of the needle which gives you a reading of the current.

Recently, a watchmaker in the west of England connected a lemon up to a tiny motor, using copper and zinc plates inserted into the lemon. This lemon powered the motor for over a year during which time it revolved over 63 000 000 times, and the lemon turned very wrinkly and black.

You could make a more powerful battery with your teacher at school. Pour an electrolyte, dilute hydrochloric acid, into a large beaker until it is half-full. Immerse a large copper plate in the beaker and place a zinc plate of the same size at the other end (fig 3). The metals must not make contact. Connect a 1.5V light bulb between the two metals (fig 4), and it lights up. After a while the light goes out, but you can prevent this by adding a small amount of potassium dichromate solution. You will notice a bubbling at the zinc plate because a gas is building up that prevents the current flowing properly. The potassium dichromate removes the gas, and your bulb should keep alight for quite a long time.

In these experiments you have generated 'current electricity', which is electricity that flows or moves.

Current electricity consists of a flow of tiny charged particles called electrons, and a flow of electrons through a lamp will make it light up. In other experiments in this book – 'The Superhuman Shock Machine' (page 9) and 'Bending Water' (page 10) you produced static electricity where the electrons do not flow but remain in approximately one position. These are the two types of electricity. Current electricity is the kind we use for lighting, heating and other forms of energy; we cannot use static electricity for these purposes.

The Crystal Forest ★★ S

You will need

a large coffee jar
a supply of water-glass (sodium silicate)
stirring rod
a supply of any of the following crystals:
    cobalt (II) chloride†
    chromium (III) sulphate†
    manganese (II) sulphate†
    iron (III) chloride†
    nickel (II) sulphate†
    copper (II) sulphate†
    aluminium (III) potassium sulphate†
spatula

What happens
You create a miniature 'tropical forest' with trees, flowers, rivers and mountains of all shapes, sizes and colours in about twenty minutes.

Pour the syrupy water-glass into the coffee jar so that it just covers the bottom, then pour water into the jar until about half-full. Shake and stir so that the water and water-glass mix well, and leave to stand for about five minutes. Use the spatula, *not* your fingers, to drop a few crystals of each chemical into the coffee jar, then sit back and watch. Your forest will start to grow almost immediately.

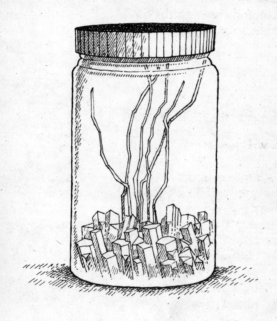

The chemical process behind the growth of this forest is very complicated and it starts with the microscopic structure of the water-glass. The water-glass forms a fine porous skin around each crystal, which allows water to enter the crystal making it swell and burst. This releases extra surfaces of crystal and more water enters. This process repeats itself until all the crystals are used up and have 'grown' into a forest.

The forest is very fragile and will crumble on the slightest movement, so do not shake or move the coffee jar.

† The figures contained in these chemicals' names refer to the oxidation states of the metals contained in the chemicals and are necessary so that the correct chemical reagent can be identified. Your teacher will explain what this means.

TYING YOURSELF IN KNOTS SOLUTION

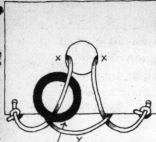

2/ FIRST PUSH THE RING THROUGH THE LOOP (Y). PULL THE STRING AT BOTH SIDES OF THE HOLE (X).

3/ THE LOOP (Y) WILL COME THROUGH THE HOLE.

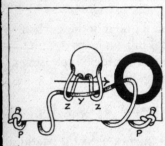

4/ BY GENTLY PULLING THE LOOPS (Z) YOU CAN PUSH THE RING THROUGH THEM.

5/ PULL GENTLY ON THE TWO LOOPS NEAR THE KNOTS. THE LOOP (Y) WILL GO BACK THROUGH THE HOLE.

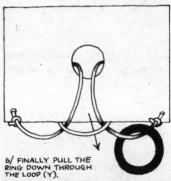

6/ FINALLY PULL THE RING DOWN THROUGH THE LOOP (Y).

THE TRICK IS TO MOVE THE STRING, NOT THE RING !

Glossary

Here is a list of some of the words that appear in this book with a simple explanation of their meaning. An 's' at the side of the word means it is found in school.

Beaker A glass or plastic container for chemicals. You could use a plastic cup instead of a beaker.

Bicarbonate of soda You'll find it in the kitchen because it's used for baking – it helps dough to rise. It produces fizz in lemonade by releasing the gas, carbon dioxide.

Boss (s) A grip on a retort stand to hold a clamp.

Bunsen burner (s) A gas burner used for heating chemicals.

Campden tablet A tablet that releases a gas to poison bacteria.

Citric acid This may be in the kitchen cupboard. It's a lemon–flavoured powder which acts as a weak acid in solution.

Clamp (s) Used on retort stands. Clamps provide a support for test-tubes, etc.

Cobalt chloride crystals (s) Crystals that are red in water and blue when dry.

Connecting wires Electrical wires connecting the various parts of an electric circuit.

Copper sulphate crystals (s) Blue crystals which dissolve in water and act as an electrolyte for 'copper-plating'.

Crocodile clips Metal clips, shaped like the jaws of a crocodile, that make connections in an electric circuit.

Crystal earplug An electronic part like a tiny loudspeaker to fit in an ear.

Crystals Solids with straight sides and regular shapes, for example, crystals of salt, sugar or copper sulphate.

Diode An electronic part used to change electricity from alternating to direct current.

Dwarf pot A flower pot which is only half the usual height.

Electrolyte A chemical which conducts electricity when dissolved in water.

Fehling's solution (s) A chemical used for experiments in biology and chemistry.

Ferrite rod aerial An electronic part found in all transistor radios.

Filter funnel Equipment used to separate solids from liquids. Often found in a kitchen.

Fuse–wire Used in plugs and circuits. Different kinds carry different currents before they burn out.

Glucose A type of sugar available at chemists.

Grow–bag A plastic bag full of a peat-based mixture ideal for growing plants in. Sold by most garden shops.

Heat–proof mat A mat made from a flat piece of insulator, like wood, which protects surfaces from heat.

Hydrochloric acid (s) A powerful acid in the laboratory.

Insulated wire Connecting wire which is covered with a plastic material to give protection against electric shocks.

Insulating tape A sticky tape for sealing and covering electric wires.

Lycopodium powder (s) A very fine light powder.

Milliammeter (s) An instrument that measures very small electric currents.

Moss peat A type of soil made of dead plants and sold in most garden shops.

Potassium dichromate (s) Orange-coloured crystals found in most laboratories in solution.

Retort stand (s) A tall metal stand for supporting instruments.

Spatula A kind of spoon for scooping up small measures of powder or crystals. An old spoon would do.

Stirring rod A glass or plastic rod for stirring. You could use an old spoon.

Test tube A small glass container for holding chemicals used in experiments.

Tripod (s) A metal stand with three legs.

Water-glass (s) A syrupy liquid used in the 'Crystal Forest' experiment. Also known as 'isinglass'.

Useful Addresses

The Secretary
Carnivorous Plant
   Society
3 Woodlands Close
London NW11 9QP

For useful information
on growing plants
which eat animals.
Young members
especially welcome. Send
SAE for details.

Marston Exotics
Marston Mill
Spring Gardens
Frome
Somerset
BA11 2NZ

Suppliers of over 100
different types of
carnivorous plants by
mail order. Catalogues
available or price list
if you send a stamped
addressed envelope.

Harold Weiner
Kaiserstrasse 74
3250 Hameln 1
West Germany

Another supplier of
many different types of
carnivorous plants.
For a price list send a
self-addressed envelope
and 2 international
reply coupons from the
post office.

Boots the Chemist
(various branches)

Supply all the various
ingredients and
equipment for making
home-made wine.

Watford Electronics
35 Cardiff Road
Watford
Herts

Supply all the parts for
the home-made radio
and will supply by
mail order.

Any hardware or electrical store will supply most
electrical equipment.

More Beaver Books

We hope you have enjoyed this Beaver Book. Here are some of the other titles:

It Figures!   A Beaver original. Did you know that you can make four 4s equal 64, add five odd numbers to make a total of 14, or multiply a three-digit number so the answer is the number repeated twice? This book is crammed with incredible calculations, tricks and games with numbers, to baffle and amaze your friends and keep you amused for hours. Written by Clive Dickinson and illustrated by Graham Thompson

The Beaver Book of Bikes   A Beaver original. Packed with information on everything you need to know about bicycles – from buying, maintenance and restoration to games, activities and the history of bikes – this book is written by Harry Hossent and illustrated with drawings by Peter Gregory and cartoons by Maggie Ling

The Missing Man   Pat Denby is the young son of a local detective, and what he sees and hears when he is out fishing one winter night puts his life in grave danger in this exciting thriller by Roderic Jefferies

These and many other Beavers are available from your local bookshop or newsagent, or can be ordered direct from: Hamlyn Paperback Cash Sales, PO Box 11, Falmouth, Cornwall TR10 9EN. Send a cheque or postal order made payable to the Hamlyn Publishing Group, for the price of the book plus postage at the following rates:
UK: 45p for the first book, 20p for the second book, and 14p for each additional book ordered to a maximum charge of £1.63;
BFPO and Eire: 45p for the first book, 20p for the second book, plus 14p per copy for the next 7 books and thereafter 8p per book;
OVERSEAS: 75p for the first book and 21p for each extra book.

New Beavers are published every month and if you would like the *Beaver Bulletin*, a newsletter which tells you about new books and gives a complete list of titles and prices, send a large stamped addressed envelope to:

Beaver Bulletin
The Hamlyn Group
Astronaut House
Feltham
Middlesex TW14 9AR

204561